Railway Clearing House

Atlas of England & Wales 1904

Ian Allan
PUBLISHING

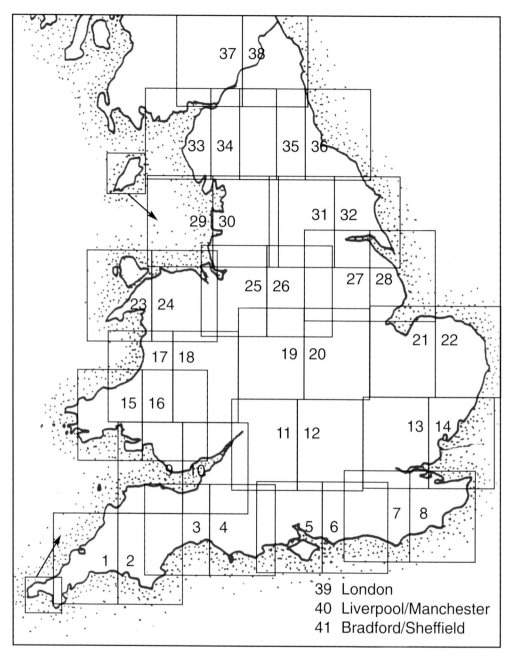

39 London
40 Liverpool/Manchester
41 Bradford/Sheffield

First published 1904 by the Railway Clearing House
This impression 2001 by Ian Allan Publishing
Reprinted 2005

ISBN 0 7110 2778 1

© this impression Ian Allan Publishing 2001

Published by Ian Allan Publishing

an imprint of Ian Allan Publishing Ltd, Hersham, Surrey KT12 4RG.

Printed in England by Ian Allan Printing Ltd, Hersham, Surrey KT12 4RG.

Code: 0504/A1

INTRODUCTION

This, the third in Ian Allan Publishing's new series of railway atlases, reproduces the 1904 edition of the Railway Clearing House *Official Railway Map of England & Wales*.

The Railway Clearing House (RCH) was established in 1842 to facilitate inter-company payments for through traffic when more than one of the many separate independent railways, eventually numbering in excess of 120, was involved. For this, accurate maps of lines owned by each company, with detailed distances, were required. George Bradshaw produced early maps between 1839 and 1845 but then concentrated on timetables. An RCH employee, Zachary Macaulay, then produced the first station map in 1851, issued by Smith & Ebbs, with subsequent editions; a list of stations was also produced. From 1862 two further employees, Henry Oliver and John Bockett, developed this into the *Handbook of Stations*, which continued, produced by Oliver and Airey (see below), from 1872.

John Airey, another employee, broadened the range of maps, producing books of Junction diagrams, including distances, from the mid-1850s up until 1894. In 1895 he sold his business to the RCH, which continued production until 1935. Airey also produced a small map of England and Wales in 1877. In 1896, the RCH produced a large map of the railways of England and Wales, this time in association with McCorquodale, which continued until the 14th edition of 1947. For a detailed history of the maps of Macaulay, Airey and the RCH see *Railway Maps and the Railway Clearing House*, published by Brunel University Library in 1986.

The 1904 issue was the fourth edition and, like the previous three, was engraved on copper by J. P. Emslie but printed from lithographic stones.

Whilst at this time the last complete main line to be built (prior to the Channel Tunnel Rail Link early in the 21st century), the Great Central main line from Marylebone, had just opened, there were still some main-line cut-offs, local lines and light railways under construction or being planned. In some cases these are included on the map (such as the PB&M — Padstow, Bedruthan & Mawgan) but were never, in actual fact, constructed.

The map was produced in colour to a scale of 7.5 miles to the inch (1:475,200) as 48 sheets on a cloth back, so that it could be folded flat, between hard covers. These sheets have been assembled and compiled into an atlas format, but, where the pages do not match the original sheets, there may be some inconsistencies, and an index is now provided. Open stations are shown in bold, goods locations in light type, and station names are as in use in 1904. Proposed railways were shown with hatched lines in the appropriate colour of the company concerned. Each railway was shown in a distinctive colour, but some colours are reused elsewhere in the country. The main railways were coloured as follows: Cambrian — purple; CLC — orange; Furness — blue; GCR — pink; GER — purple; GNR — orange; GWR — yellow; H&B — purple; L&YR — blue; LB&SCR — green; LD&ECR — blue; LNWR — red; LSWR — blue; LT&SR — yellow; M&GNR — yellow; MR — green; Metropolitan — light blue; NBR — blue; NER — yellow; NSR — purple; SECR — pink. Other independent and light railways were shown in various colours as appropriate. Joint railways received hatched lines in the colours of the owning companies.

A list of railway abbreviations not explained fully on the maps will be found on p45.

1   2   3   4   5

A

PORTREATH
GOODS
Godrevy
St IVES
St Ives
Bay
CARBIS BAY
WNEAL
CROFTY
ROSKEAR
CARN
BREA
CAMBORNE
REDRU
SCORRIER
LELANT
HAYLE
GWINEAR
ROAD
HARVEY
PRAZE
TRESA
STERTH
MARAZION
PENZANCE
G.W.
NANCEGOLLAN
Newlyn
St Michael's
Mount
Mount's Bay
Perranuthnoe
Consta
B
Mousehole
HELSTON
Porthleven
Loo Pool
Ma
COACH ROAD
gan Rock
Mullion
Mullion I.
Ku

Sharpnose
Morwinstow
R. Tamar
Pu

Bude
Bay
BUDE
QUAY
STRATION
STA R.
HOLSW

C
Dazard Pt
Cambeak
St Gennys
WHITSTONE
& BRIDGERULE
N. Tamerton

Boscastle
TRESMEER
Tintagel
OTTERHAM
CAMELFORD
EGLOSKERRY
L & S.W.
LAUNC

Port Isaac
Bay
L. & S.W.
DELABOLE
Brown Willy
Altarnun
L.

Pentire Pt
Padstow Bay
Port
Isaac
PORT ISAAC
ROAD
Bodmin
Moor
North H

D
PADSTOW
QUAY
R. Camel
WENFORD
BRIDGE
STONS
MINE
Cheesewring
St KEW
HIGHWAY
STH CARADON
MINE
WADEBRIDGE
R. Camel
C.

Mawgan Porth
GROGLEY JUNC.
L & S.W.
BODMIN
DOUBLEBOIS
MOORSWATER
CARADON
MAWGAN
RUTHERN BRIDGE
BOSCARNE
JUNC.
G.W.
LISKEARD
Towan He d
BODMIN
ROAD
COOMBE
NEWQUAY
STA
St COLUMB Rd
St DENNIS Jn
BUGLE
LOSTWITHIEL
St KEYNE
MENHE
E
Penhale Pt
G.W.
VICTORIA
CARBUS
BRIDGES
CAUSELAND
LISKEARD
& LOOE
GRAVE HILL
MELANGOOSE MILL
CAUDLEDOWN
CLEAVES
SANDPLACE
SAINT GE
Perran
Bay
TREAMBLE
DRINNICK
MILL
GUNNESTHORP
COLANT
NEWLYN EAST
BURNGULLOW
CARBEAN
St
BLAZEY
PAR
LOOE
St Agnes Hd
PERRANPORTH
GRAMPOUND
ROAD
CARBEAN
St
AUSTELL
YOPE'S
HARBOUR
DOCK
FOWEY
Looe I.
St AGNES
(Gauge 2. 6)
GOON
PIER
F
CHACEWATER
GREAT
WESTERN
ROAD
St Austell
Bay
Polperro
EATH
DS
SCORRIER
TRURO
NEWHAM
GOODS
TREGONY
PENTEWAN
Mevagissey
Fowey R.
WNEAL
CROFTY
AR
REDRUTH
PERRITH
JUNC
R. Fal
CARN
BREA
P RRAN ELL
Veryan
Veryan
B.
Dodman Pt
CAMBORNE
TRESAVEAN
O
Nare Hd
G
PENRYN
St MAWES
FALMOUTH
Constantine
Falmouth
Bay
Zoze Pt
HELSTON

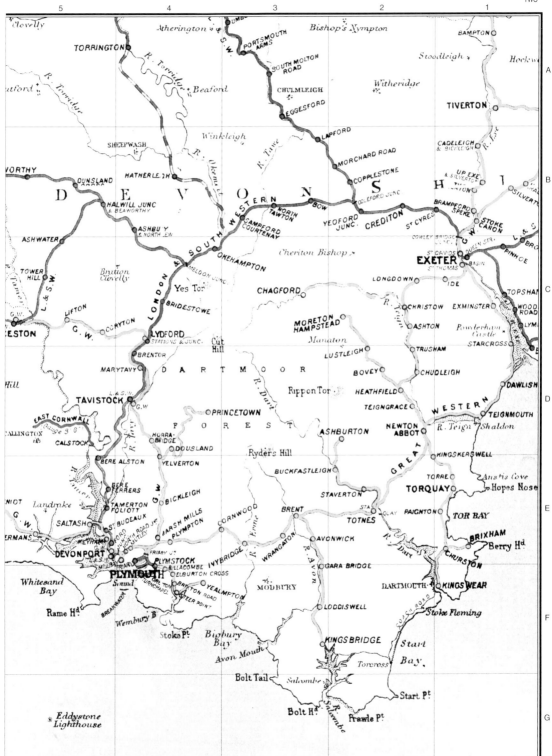

1   2   3   4   5

Porlock
Porlock
Road
OR
Dunkery Beacon
S T
Exford
Brendon Hills
Exton
MINEHEAD
DUNSTER
BLUE ANCHOR
WASHFORD
WATCHET
G.W.
WILLITON
ROADWATER
GUPWORTHY
W. SOMERSET
COMBE ROW
RALEIGH'S CROSS

B a y
BOURNHAM
KNOLL
HIGHBRIDGE
DRAYCOTT
Wedmore
LODGE HILL
Nether Stowey
DUNBALL
BACON BRIDGE
COSSINGTON
EDINGTON
SHAPWICK
ASHCOTT
GLASTO
& STR
R. Brue
POL

Quantock Hills
STOGUMBER
CROWCOMBE
BRIDGWATER
G.W.
WHARF
S.&D.
DOCKS
Polden Hills
Sedge Moor
CHA
SOMERTON

B
S NYMPTON
EAST ANSTEY
CULVERTON
MOREBATH
VENN CROSS
Huish Champflower
WIVELISCOMBE
BISHOP'S LYDEARD
North Petherton
DURSTON
ATHELNEY
LANGPORT
R.
ILCHE

BAMPTON
MILVERTON
TAUNTON
NORTON FITZWARREN
CREECH JUNC
THORNFALCON
R. Tone

Stoodleigh
Hockworthy
Blackdown Hills
WELLINGTON
Coate
HATCH
SOUTH PETHERTON
MARTOCK
MONTACUTE
G.W.
R. Parret

C
itheridge
GREAT WESTERN
BURLES COMBE
HEMYOCK
CULMSTOCK
UFFCULME
ILMINSTER
Hinton St George
CREWKERNE

TIVERTON
TIVERTON JUNC
CADELEIGH & BICKLEIGH
CULLOMPTON
Up Otter
CHARD
G.W.
L.&S.W.
JOINT
POINT

ROAD
STONE
UP EXE & SILVERTON
BRADNINCH
SILVERTON
HELE & BRADNINCH
HONITON
CHARD JUNC
Pillesdon Pen
D

D
DITON
JUNC
BRAMPFORD SPEKE
ST CYRES
STOKE CANON
COWLEY BRIDGE
QUEEN STR
G.W.
L.&S.W.
WHIMPLE
SIDMOUTH JUNC
OTTERY ST MARY
SEATON JUNC
R. Axe
AXMINSTER
A.&L.R.
POWERST
HIRE

St DAVIDS
EXETER
St THOMAS
BASIN
PINHOE
BROAD CLYST
TIPTON ST JOHN'S
COLYTON TOWN
COLYFORD
SEATON
LIGHT
COMBPYNE
LYME REGIS
Charmouth
EAST STREET
STA
BRI
WEST

NGDOWN
IDE
TOPSHAM
NEWTON POPPLEFORD
SIDMOUTH
Beer
Beer Hd
Bridport Harb

E
R.
CHRISTOW
EXMINSTER
WOODBURY ROAD
EAST BUDLEIGH
Powderham Castle
LYMPSTONE
LITTLEHAM
BUDLEIGH SALTERTON
ASHTON
TRUSHAM
STARCROSS
EXMOUTH
Straight Pt

FIELD
CHUDLEIGH
DAWLISH
NGRACE
WESTERN
TEIGNMOUTH
NEWTON ABBOT
R. Teign
Shaldon
GREAT
KINGSKERSWELL

TORRE
Anstis Cove
Hopes Nose
TORQUAY
PAIGNTON
TOR BAY
CLAY
BRIXHAM
Berry Hd
R. Dart

5   4   3   2   1

CHILCOMPTON
BINEGAR
VOBSTER
FROME

S A L I S B U
Durrington
BUL
AME

A

LOW.
WELLS
GW. S&D.
COOKEY
GW.
SHAM

G. W.
MASBURY
S&D
CRANMORE
SHEPTON MALLET
WARMINSTER

Longleat Park
R. WYLE
HEYTESBURY

P L A I
NEWTON

SOMERSET
WANSTROW
WITHAM
GRT. WESTERN
CODFORD
WYLYE
WISHFORD
RT WESTERN

WILTON
GT.
L&SW.
L.&S.W.
SALISBURY

B

NBURY
REET
PENNARD
PYLLE
EVERCREECH
NEW!
S&D.
EVERCREECH
JUNC.

CASTLE CARY
Alfred's Tower
BRUTON
Stourton
MERE
HINDON
Fonthill Abbey
TISBURY
DINTON
Broad Chalk

FOSSEWAY
COLE
R. Stour
SEMLEY
Wardour Castle

RLTON
WINCANTON
DORSET

SPARKFORD
SOUTH WESTERN
GILLINGHAM
Cranborne Chase
Martin
L.&S.W.
BREA
C

Yeo
ESTER
MARSTON MAGNA
MILBORNE PORT
S&D.
L&SW.
SHAFTESBURY
Fontmell Magna
CRANBORNE
VERWOOD
FORDINGBR

PEN MILL TOWN
HENDFORD GOODS
LONDON
HENSTRIDGE
STALBRIDGE
L.&S.W.
CRANBORNE
DAGGON'S ROAD
R. Arm

YEOVIL
JUNC. STA.
SHERBORNE
STURMINSTER NEWTON
MID JOINT
Pimperne
Witchampton
RINGWO

SUTTON BINGHAM
CLIFTON MAYBANK GOODS
YETMINSTER
SHILLINGSTONE
R. Stour

Dorset
H e i g h t s
R S E
WEST MOORS
H

O
EVERSHOT
CERNE ABBAS
Milton Abbas
BLANDFORD
WIMBORNE
Tench's Ford
D

TOLLER
MAIDEN NEWTON
SPETISBURY
STA.
HORN
ADMI

STOCK
GRIMSTONE & FRAMPTON
PIDDLETOWN
BERE REGIS
BAILEY GATE
OROADSTONE
JUNC. STA.
BOSCOMBE
CHRIS

DPORT BAY
DORCHESTER
L&SW.
R. Frome
L&SW
WAREHAM
HAMWORTHY JUNC.
HAMWORTHY
POOLE
PARKSTONE
BRANKSOME
BOURNEMOUTH
CENTRAL
Southbourn

Punchnoll
PORTESHAM
MORETON
WOOL
Poole Hr.
E

ABBOTSBURY
BROADWEY
UPWEY
Osmington
WORGRET JUNC.
Studland
Foreland

The Fleet
Chesil Bank
Lulworth Cove
Purbeck Hills
CORFE CASTLE
SWANAGE

JUNC. STA.
WEYMOUTH
HARBOUR STA.
Weymouth Bay
Worbarrow Bay
Durlestone Pt.

RODWELL
Portld Road
BREAKWATER
St. Albans Hd.

PORTLAND
West Bay
EASTON
CASTLETON LOADING PLACE
Portland Isle
F

Portland Bill

G

1   2   3   4   5

DEVIZES

Potterne

GREAT WESTERN
PEWSEY

BURBAGE

WOODHAY
Newtown

MORTIM

Silchester

A

PATNEY
& CHIRTON

WOODBOROUGH

GRAFTON

HIGHCLERE

KINGSCLERE

BRAMLEY

G.W.

WOOLHILL

WOODHAY
Newtown

CLAVINGTON

Upavon

Everleigh

COLINGBOURNE

Hurstbourne
Tarrant

BURGHCLERE

LITCHFIELD

OVERTON

OAKLEY

Sherborne
St John

BASINGSTOKE

WORTHING

G.W.

TIDWORTH

Durrington

L   I   S   B   U   R   Y

WEYHILL

LUDGERSHALL

HURSTBOURNE

SUTTON
SCCTNEY

CUDDESDEN

B

BULFORD

STONEHENGE

WESTERN

SOUTH

JUNC STA
HD LODGES

ANDOVER
TOWN STA

CLATFORD

LONG
PARISH

R Junction

WHITCHURCH

WESTERN

MICHELDEVER

HERRIARD

Preston
Candover
& LAS

AMESBURY

GRATELEY

&

WHERWELL

SOUTH

BENTWC
& LAS

P   L   A   I   N

NEWTON TONEY

LONDON

FULLERTON

East Stratton

WYLYE

Walleys

EAST STRATTON

MEDSTEAD

GRT WESTERN

WISHFORD

PORTON

STOCKBRIDGE

Crawley

L. & S.W.

JUNC.

L. & S. W.

ITCHEN ABBAS

ROPLEY

WILTON

L.&.S.W.

GODES

Wintershow

HORSEBRIDGE

WINCHESTER

O G. W.
JUNC.

ALRESFORD

C

ONTON

SALISBURY

ALDERBURY
JUNC

DEAN

MOTTISFONT

LONDON

SHAWFORD
& TWYFORD

Cheriton

WEST MEON

Broad Chalk

DUNBRIDGE
KIMBRIDGE
JUNC

Hursley

&

Cranborne
Chase

Martin

DOWNTON

ROMSEY

CHANDLERS
FORD

Upham

S

D

CRANBORNE

L. & S. W.

BREAMORE

Bramshaw

NURSLING

SWAYTHLING

EASTLEIGH
& BISHOPSTOKE

BISHOPS
WALTHAM

DROXFOR
FOR NAMSLEDO

FORDINGBRIDGE

REDBRIDGE
TOTTON

SOUTHAMPTON

BOTLEY

Ham

DAGGENS ROAD

Rufus Stone

N   e   w

LYNDHURST
ROAD

WOOLSTON
SHOLING

WICKHAM

Fores

VERWOOD

Lyndhurst

BITTERNE

NETTLEY

R Hamble

Witchampton

RINGWOOD

F   o   r   e   s   t

BEAULIEU
ROAD

MILLBROOK
WEST STA

NORTHAM

CHESTER

BURSLEDON

PORTCHESTER

COSH

WEST MOORS

H

Beaulieu

Hythe

SWANWICK

FAREHAM

L. & S. W.

E

WIMBORNE

HOLMSLEY

New Hurst

Tyrrels
Ford

NEW MILTON

HINTON
ADMIRAL

S WAY

BROCKENHURST

FAWLEY

Stone Pt

BROCKENHURST

ISLE OF

PORT

Spithead

PARKSTONE

BROADSTONE
JUNC. STA.

FORESOWN

BOSCOMBE

L. & S W

Burton
on Sea

LYMINGTON
STA
PIER

COWES
STA

MILL

Osborne

BAY

Spithead

POOLE

HAM
WORTHY

JUNC R Stour

HURN

BOURNEMOUTH
CENTRAL

Southbourne
on Sea

CHRISTCHURCH

Milford
on Sea

Hurst Castle

T   H   E

S   O   L   E   N   T

YARMOUTH

WHIPPINGHAM

PIER HEAD
ESPLANADE

RYDE

ST JOHNS ROAD

SMALLBROOK JU

BE

F

Poole H?

BRANKSOME

Bengistbury Hd

Totland B.

NEWPORT

WOOTTON

ST HELENS

Studland

Foreland

Alum B.

FRESHWATER

The Needles

Freshwater
Bay

CALBOURNE
& SHALFLEET

F. & N.

RINGWOOD

CARISBROOKE

SHIDE

HAVEN
STREET

ASHEY

BRADING

Brighstone

BLACKWATER

MERSTONE

NEWCHURCH

ALVERSTON

SANDOWN

SWANAGE

ISLE OF WIGHT

HORRINGFORD

ISLE OF W

SHANKLIN

G

Durlestone Pt

GODSHILL

WROXALL

WHITWELL

TOWN

St Catherine P?

ST
LAWRENCE

Undercliff

VENTNOR

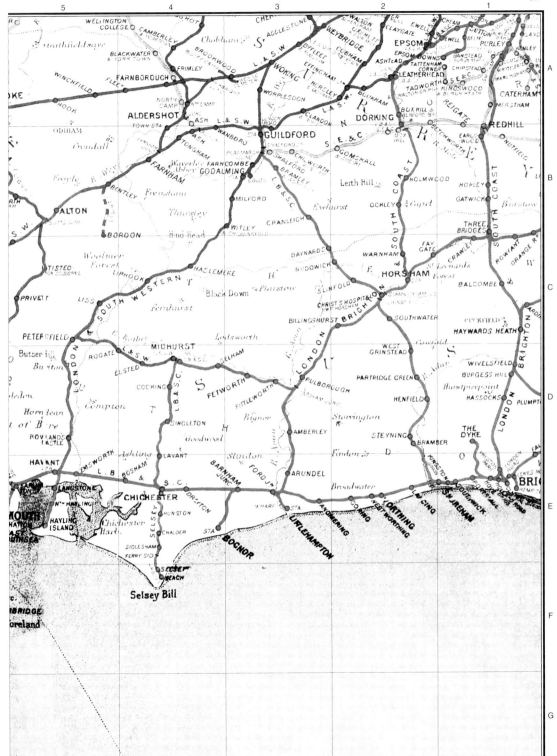

Selsey Bill

1   2   3   4   5

A

LONDON

TILBURY & SOUTHEND

Langdon Hill

Canvey I.

SOUTH END ON

THAMES HAVEN

RIVER THAM

STRATFORD
BARKING
BECKTON
RAINHAM
DAGENHAM
PURFLEET
GRAYS
TILBURY DOCK
CLIFFE
CHARNAL STREET

WOOLWICH
BELVEDERE
ERITH
GREENWICH
GRAVESEND
STROOD
ROCHESTER
CHATHAM

B

CROYDON
BROMLEY
ORPINGTON
SWANLEY
CHATHAM
CUXTON
HALLING
SNODLAND
AYLESFORD
SITTINGBOURNE
BEARSTED
NEWINGTON
RAINHAM

C

DOWNS
CATERHAM
REDHILL
WESTERHAM
SEVENOAKS
Knole Park
Mereworth
WEST MAIDSTONE
EAST FARLEIGH
HARRIETSHAM
LENHAM
Sutton Valence

D

OXTED
EDENBRIDGE
TONBRIDGE
SOUTH EASTERN
HORLEY
GATWICK
LINGFIELD
DORMANS
HEVER
COWDEN
PENSHURST
SOUTHBORO
PADDOCK WOOD
MARDEN
STAPLEHURST
HEADCORN
FRITTENDEN ROAD
BIDD
THREE BRIDGES
EAST GRINSTEAD
ASHURST
GROOMBRIDGE
TUNBRIDGE WELLS
FRANT
GOUDHURST
CRANBROOK

E

FAY GATE
CRAWLEY
GRANGE Rd.
KINGSCOTE
HARTFIELD
WITHYHAM
WADHURST
HAWKHURST
ROLVENDEN
BALCOMBE
WEST HOATHLY
HORSTED KEYNES
CROWBOROUGH
Ashdown Forest
MAYFIELD
TICEHURST ROAD
ETCHINGHAM
ROTHER VALLEY
BODIAM
HAYWARDS HEATH
ARDINGLY
SHEFFIELD PARK
Maresfield
Burwash
ROBERTSBRIDGE
JUNCTION ROAD
WIVELSFIELD
NEWICK & CHAILEY
BUXTED
HEATHFIELD
Dallington
BURGESS HILL
UCKFIELD
WALDRON
BATTLE
WINCHE

F

HASSOCKS
PLUMPTON
BAR COMBE
ISFIELD
BARCOMBE MILLS
East Hoathly
HELLINGLEY
CROWHURST
THE DYKE
COOKS BRIDGE
Laughton
Herstmonceux
WEST ST LEONARDS
FALMER
LEWES
GLYNDE
HAILSHAM
BEXHILL
HASTINGS
BRAMBER
BERWICK
PEVENSEY
ST. LEONARDS
SHOREHAM
SOUTHWICK
PORTSLADE
BRIGHTON
ROTTINGDEAN
POLEGATE
Pevensey Bay
HAMPDEN PARK

G

NEWHAVEN
SEAFORD
BISHOPSTONE
EASTBOURNE
Cuckmere Haven
Beachy Head

5 4 3 2 1

A

B

C

D

E

F

G

PRITTLEWELL
Maplin Sand
SHOEBURYNESS
HEND
SEA
Pier
Shoebury Ness

Nore Light

To Flushing

Margate Sand

YARD
SHEERNESS
SHEERNESS ON SEA
SHEERNESS
EAST MINSTER ON SEA
PIER
EAST MINSTER
ENBOROUGH
SHEPPEY
EASTCHURCH
Warden Pt
MARGATE
SANDS
Foreness
MARGATE
North Foreland
LEYSDOWN
Isle of Sheppey
HERNE BAY
S.E. & C.
BIRCHINGTON
WESTGATE
BROADSTAIRS
WHITSTABLE
HARBOUR
TOWN
St LAWRENCE
RAMSGATE
MILTON Swale
MINSTER
HARBOUR
URNE
GRUVE FERRY
Penwell Bay
TEYNHAM
STURRY
Stour
Goodwin Sands
Boughton
Pegwell Bay
URNE
Doddington
FAVERSHAM
SELLING
WEST
CANTERBURY
SANDWICH
The
DEAL
Sheldwich
ST
BEEKESBOURNE
Eastry
Downs
CHARTHAM
Molash
CHILHAM
BRIG
ADISHAM
SHEPHERDS
WELL
WALMER
Kingsdown
S.E. & C.
BISHOPSBOURNE
BARHAM
MARTIN
MILL
St Margaret's
CHARING
Eastwell
WYE
N
Wingham S
DOVER & DEAL
South Foreland
CHATHAM
HOTHFIELD
ELHAM
KEARSNEY
PLUCKLEY
WEST
ASHFORD
Barbourne
LYMINGE
HARBOUR
DOVER
Bethersden
EAST
Sellindge
HORTON RD
TOWN
PIER
DENDEN
SMEETH
WESTENHANGER
SANDLING JUNC.
JUNC. STA.
HIGH HALDEN
HAM STREET
HYTHE
CENTRAL
HARBOUR
FOLKESTONE
SANDGATE
TENTERDEN
TOWN
APPLEDORE
Romney
Dymchurch
Marsh
TTERSHAM
ROAD
BROOKLAND
NEW ROMNEY &
LITTLESTONE ON SEA
Walland
Marsh
RYE
LYDD
ROCAMBER
DUNGENESS
Dunge Ness
LSEA
HARBOUR
Rye Bay

DOVER STRAIT

C. Blan

C. Gris Nez

BOULOGNE

1   2   3   4   5

A

BRYN AMMAN
LLANDEBIE
GLANAMMAN
CARNANT
PENWYLLT
CWM AMAN
CROSS HANDS
PONTYBEREM
TIRYDAIL
AMMANFORD
ABERCRAVE
GWYS
COLBREN JUNC
ONLLWYN
FERRYSIDE
TUMBLE
PANTYFFYNNON
GURNOS
YSTRAD GYNLAIS
SEVEN SISTERS
MAESMARCHOG COL
PONT YEAT
CWM BLAWD
YNYS Y GWSINON JUNC
KIDWELLY
PONTARDULAIS
PONTARDAWE
MIDLAND
NEATH & BRECON
CRYNANT
GLYN NEATH
HIRWAIN
ME
LLWYDCOED
PEMBREY & BURRY PORT
LLAN-GENNECH
GAFEN
GLYDACH ON TAWE
CILFREW
RESOLVEN
BLAEN PHONCHA
ABERDARE
LLANELLY
BYNEA
GLAIS
NEATH ABBEY
GW
GREAT WESTERN
TREHERBERT
MAERDY
Burry Inlet
PENCWDD
GORSEINON
MORRISTON
LANDORE
DYNEVOR
LLAN SAMLET
NEATH
BRITON FERRY
CYMMER
CAERAU
NANTYMOEL
FFALDAU

B

GOWERTON
DUNVANT
HIGH ST
ROTLAND ST
PORT
RHYDYFEN
AVON R&SB
CWM
PORT TALBOT
TRUEDYRHIEW GARTH
PONTY CYMMER
OGMORE VALE
POR
Burry Holmes
LLANMORLIS
KILLAY
MUMBLES ROAD
SWANSEA
ABERAVON
SEA SIDE
DOCKS
LLANGONOYD
LLETTY BRONGU
LLANGEINOR
BLACK MILL
Rhossilly Bay
GOWER
MUMBLES
Swansea Bay
PORT TALBOT J.
MARGAM
BRYNMENYN LLANHARAN
Worms Head
Rhossilly
MUMBLES Hd
PYLE
WESTERN
PENCOED
LLANTRISA

C

Helwick Shoals
Portynon
Caswell B.
GREAT
BRIDGEND
LLANHARRY
PORTH CAWL
HARBOUR STA
COITY JUNC
YSTRADOWEN
SOUTHERNDOWN ROAD
COWBRIDGE

D

B R I S T O L
Nash Point
LLANTWIT MAJOR
GILESTON

E

C H A N
The Foreland
Lynmouth
Porlock Bay

F

Widmouth Hd
LYNTON
Porlock
COACH ROAD
MINEHEAD
ILFRACOMBE
COMBE MARTIN
WOODY BAY
EXMOOR
DUNSTER
Morte Pt
MORTE OE
BLACKMOOR
Dunkery Beacon
BLUE ANCHOR
Morte Bay
Bittadon
FOREST
Simonsbath
S
Exford
WAS
Baggy Pt
LYNTON & BARNSTAPLE
BRATTON FLEMING
Span Head
GURWORTHY
W. SOMERSE
BRAUNTON
CHELFHAM
Brendo
BARNSTAPLE
WRAFTON
BARNSTAPLE
Exton

G

BAY
APPLEDORE
NORTHAM
INSTOW
FRENG TO
SWIMBRIDGE
FILLEIGH
GREAT
SOUTH MOLTON
BISHOP'S NYMPTON
EAST ANSTEY
CULVERTON
MOREBATH
WESTWARD HO!
ABBOTSHAM ROAD
BIDEFORD
CHAPELTON
WESTERN
Clovelly
therington
UMBERLEIGH
Bishop's Nympton
BAMPTON

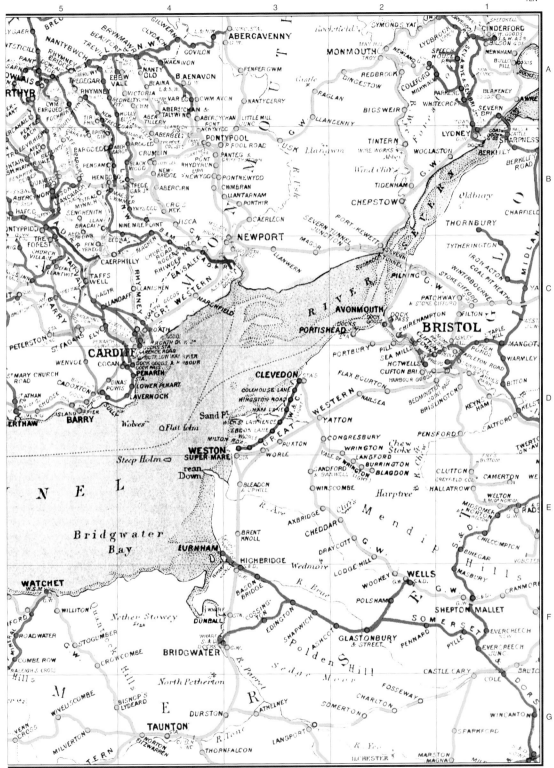

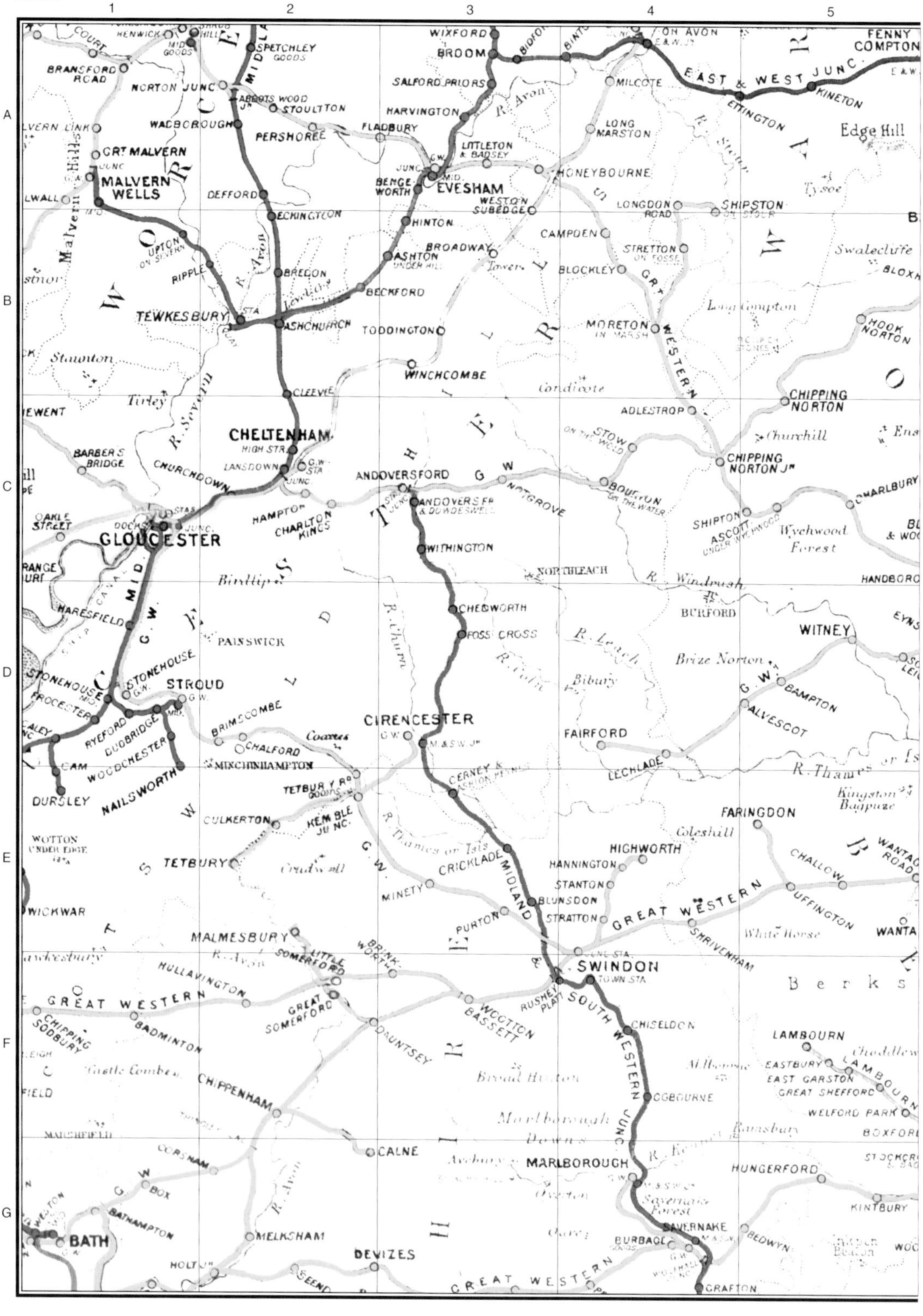
1
2
3
4
5
A
B
C
D
E
F
G
HENWICK
SPETCHLEY GOODS
BRANSFORD ROAD
NORTON JUNC
ABBOTS WOOD JN
STOULTTON
WADBOROUGH
PERSHORE
GRT MALVERN
MALVERN WELLS
DEFFORD
ECKINGTON
UPTON ON SEVERN
RIPPLE
TEWKESBURY
ASHCHURCH
BREDON
BECKFORD
R. Avon
Malvern Hills
Staunton
Tirley
R. Severn
CLEEVE
CHELTENHAM
HIGH STR.
LANSDOWN
CHURCHDOWN
BARBER'S BRIDGE
OAKLE STREET
GLOUCESTER
DOCKS
MID.
G.W.
HARESFIELD
PAINSWICK
STONEHOUSE
STROUD
FROCESTER
RYEFORD
DUDBRIDGE
WOODCHESTER
NAILSWORTH
CAM
DURSLEY
BRIMSCOMBE
CHALFORD
MINCHINHAMPTON
WOTTON UNDER EDGE
TETBURY
CULKERTON
KEMBLE JUNC.
TETBURY RD
WICKWAR
MALMESBURY
LITTLE SOMERFORD
GREAT SOMERFORD
HULLAVINGTON
GREAT WESTERN
BADMINTON
CHIPPING SODBURY
DAUNTSEY
CHIPPENHAM
CALNE
CORSHAM
BOX
BATHAMPTON
BATH
MELKSHAM
HOLT JN
DEVIZES
SEEND
WIXFORD
BROOM
SALFORD PRIORS
HARVINGTON
FLADBURY
LITTLETON & BADSEY
EVESHAM
BENGEWORTH
HINTON
ASHTON UNDER HILL
BROADWAY
TODDINGTON
WINCHCOMBE
ANDOVERSFORD
ANDOVERSFD & DOWDESWELL
HAMPTON
CHARLTON KINGS
NOTGROVE
WITHINGTON
CHEDWORTH
FOSS CROSS
R. Churn
CIRENCESTER
M. & S.W. JN
CERNEY & ASHTON KEYNES
MINETY
CRICKLADE
MIDLAND
BLUNSDON
PURTON
BRINKWORTH
WOOTTON BASSETT
SWINDON
TOWN STA
RUSHEY PLATT
SOUTH WESTERN
CHISELDON
OGBOURNE
MARLBOROUGH
Marlborough Downs
Savernake Forest
SAVERNAKE
BURBAGE
GRAFTON
GREAT WESTERN
ON AVON
EAST & WEST JUNC.
MILCOTE
LONG MARSTON
HONEYBOURNE
WESTON SUBEDGE
CAMPDEN
BLOCKLEY
LONGDON ROAD
SHIPSTON ON STOUR
STRETTON ON FOSSE
MORETON IN MARSH
Long Compton
ADLESTROP
STOW ON THE WOLD
BOURTON ON THE WATER
NORTHLEACH
R. Windrush
BURFORD
R. Leach
R. Coln
Bibury
FAIRFORD
LECHLADE
R. Thames or Isis
HIGHWORTH
HANNINGTON
STANTON
STRATTON
SHRIVENHAM
Coleshill
FARINGDON
FENNY COMPTON
ETTINGTON
KINETON
Edge Hill
Tysoe
Swalecliffe
HOOK NORTON
CHIPPING NORTON
Churchill
CHIPPING NORTON JN
SHIPTON
ASCOTT UNDER WYCHWOOD
Wychwood Forest
CHARLBURY
HANDBORO
WITNEY
Brize Norton
BAMPTON
ALVESCOT
Kingston Bagpuze
CHALLOW
UFFINGTON
White Horse
Berks
LAMBOURN
EASTBURY
EAST GARSTON
GREAT SHEFFORD
WELFORD PARK
BOXFORD
HUNGERFORD
KINTBURY
BEDWYN
Ramsbury
R. Kennet
Avebury
Broad Hinton
Overton
Oare

5   4   3   2   1

BLISWORTH
SALCEY FOREST GOODS
G.W. JUNC.
BYFIELD
WOODFORD & H'NTON
OLNEY
TURVEY
OAKLEY
WILLIN
STAT. JUNC.
MORTON PINKNEY
BLAKESLEY
BANBURY
ROADE
N.W.
STOKE BRUERN
RAVENSTONE JUNC.
BEDFORD
MID.
CARDING TON
CULWORTH JUNC.
CULWORTH
TOWCESTER
GREEN STAT. JUNC.
Hanslope
Astwood
SOU
CROPREDY
NORTHAMPTON
WAPPENHAM
NORTON
CASTLETHORPE
House
NEWPORT PAGNELL
Wootton
A
Sulgrave
N.&B.J.
HELMDON
G.C.
Whittlewood
WOLVERTON
GRT. LINFORD
MILLBROOK
LIDLINGTON
BANBURY
G.W.
L.&N.W. JUNC.
FARTHING HOE
BRACKLEY
Forest
STONY STRATFORD
BRADWELL
RIDGMONT
AMPTHILL
Si
B
ADDERBURY
KINGS SUTTON
G.C.
FULWELL & Stowe
BUCKINGHAM
Shenley
WOBURN SANDS
FLITWICK
L.&N.W.
GREAT
L.&N.W.
PADBURY
BLETCHLEY
FENNY STRATFORD
WOBURN ABBEY
HARLINGTON
DEDDINGTON
AYNHO
FINMERE
VERNEY JUNC.
SWANBOURNE
Hockliffe
HEYFORD
CENTRAL
CLAYDON
WINSLOW
B
LEIGHTON
L.&N.W.
LEAGRAVE
SOMERTON
Ardley
MARCH GIBBON & POUNDON
WINSLOW RD.
STANBRIDGE FORD
DUNSTABLE
LU
LAUNTON
WESTERN
CALVERT
GRANDBOROUGH
WING
G.N.
C
BICESTER
GRANDBOROUGH
LONDON & NTH
CHEDDINGTON
Dunstable Downs
C.N.
BLETCHINGTON
QUAINTON ROAD
WADDESDON
MARSTON GATE
LUTON H
KIDLINGTON
WESTCOTT
MET.
WADDESDON MANOR
IVINGHOE
HARPE
ISLIP
WOOD SID.
WOTTON
LONDON
REDBOUR
YARNTON
BRILL
OXFORD RD.
AYLESBURY TRAMROAD
AYLESBURY
G.W. & MET.
NORTH
HEMEL HEMPSTEAD
MID.
OXFORD JUNC.
Oakley
G.W. & MET. JOINT
STOKE MANDEVILLE
L.&N.W.
TRING
Gt. Gaddesden
E
OXFORD
HADDENHAM
WENDOVER
WESTERN
BERKHAMSTED
BOXMOOR
G.W.
L.&N.W.
THAME
LITTLE KIMBLE
II
Cumnor
GRT. WESTERN
PRINCES RISBORO
GREAT MISSENDEN
CHESHAM
KINGS LANGLEY
D
KENNINGTON JUNC.
WHEATLEY
TIDDINGTON
BLEDLOW
G.C.
Chenies
Cassiobury
RADLEY
CHINNOR
SAUNDERTON
METROPOLITAN
ABINGDON
ASTON ROWANT
Stokenchurch
AMERSHAM
CHALFONT ROAD
CHORLEY WOOD
STEVENTON
CULHAM
Dorchester
WEST WYCOMBE
Hughenden
RICKMANSWORTH
E
WATLINGTON
Benson
HIGH WYCOMBE
Penn
BEACONSFIELD
GERRARDS CROSS
NORTHWOOD
DIDCOT
Turville
LOUDWATER
WOODBURN GREEN
UPTON
WALLINGFORD
MARLOW
BOURNE END
DENHAM
PIN
CHOLSEY & MOULSFORD
Nettlebed
COOKHAM
ICKENHAM & MET.
UXBRIDGE
GRE
hire
EAST ILSLEY
CHURN
BURNHAM BEECHES
SLOUGH
WEST DRAYTON
F
COMPTON
GORING & STREATLEY
HENLEY ON THAMES
MAIDENHEAD
TAPLOW
LANGLEY
HAYES
G.W.
HAMPSTEAD NORRIS
Whitchurch
SHIPLAKE
Bray
DATCHET
COLNBROOK
PANGBOURNE
WARGRAVE
WESTERN
WINDSOR
L.&S.W.
HERMITAGE
TILEHURST
GRT.
TWYFORD
WRAYSBURY
VALLEY
READING
EARLEY
Windsor Park
STAINES
SPEEN
ALDERMASTON
THEALE
EGHAM
VIRGINIA WATER
HEPPER TON
NEWBURY
MIDGHAM
WOKINGHAM
BRACKNELL
ASCOT
SUNNINGDALE
CHERTSEY
G
THATCHAM
R. Kennet
L.&S.W.
BAGSHOT
WEYB
HIGHCLERE
MORTIMER
WELLINGTON COLLEGE
CAMBERLEY
Chobham

1   2   3   4   5

A
B
C
D
E
F
G

CAMBRIDGE
BARNWELL
DULLINGHAM
SIX MILE BOTTOM
FULBOURNE
Lidgate
OLD NORTH ROAD
CAXTON
Eltisley
Eaton Socon
TEMPSFORD
SHELFORD
HARSTON
FOXTON
SHEPRETH
WHITTLESFORD
LINTON
BARTLOW
HAVERHILL
STURMER
STONE
MELDRETH & MELBOURN
GAMLINGAY
POTTON
SANDY
BLUNHAM
L. & N.W.
BIGGLESWADE
LANGFORD
ROYSTON
Ickleton
GREAT CHESTERFORD
Heydon
Balsham
BIRDBROOK
YELDHAM
SOUTHILL
ARLESEY & SHEFFORD RD
THREE COUNTIES
ASHWELL
Barley
AUDLEY END
SAFFRON WALDEN
Radwinter
SHEFFORD
HENLOW
BALDOCK
Barkway
NEWPORT
GREAT EASTERN
Silsoe
Warden
HITCHIN
Weston
BUNTINGFORD
Clavering
Henham
NORTH ESSEX
THAXTED
Saling
BRAINT
CAST HEDING
STEVENAGE
WESTMILL
ELSENHAM
LUTON
Whitwell
Lilley
BRAUGHING
STANDON
STANSTED
DUNMOW
FELSTEAD
BRAINT
CHILTERN GREEN
KNEBWORTH
Walton
HADHAM
BISHOP'S STORTFORD
TAKELEY
EASTON LODGE
RAYNE
BULFORD
WHEATHAMPSTEAD
WELWYN
WIDFORD
SAWBRIDGEWORTH
High Easter
ARPENDEN
HERTFORD
WARE
MARDOCK
ST. MARGARET'S
HARLOW
Matching
CHELMSFORD
Writtle
Danbury
HATFIELD
RYE HOUSE
ROYDON
BURNT MILL
ST. ALBANS
HERTINGFORDBURY
BROXBOURNE
Potter Street
BLAKE HALL
ONGAR
Blackmoor
PARK STREET
Essendon
HODDESDON
NORTHWEALD
INGATESTONE
BRICKET WOOD
POTTERS BAR
THEOBALDS GROVE
CHESHUNT
EPPING
RADLETT
ELSTREE
HADLEY WOOD
WALTHAM
THEYDON BOIS
SHENFIELD & HUTTON
BATTLESBRIDG
WATFORD
BUSHEY
HIGH BARNET
NEW BARNET
ENFIELD
ENFIELD LOCK
CHIGWELL LANE
LOUGHTON
BRENTWOOD
WICKFORD
BILLERICAY
GRT. EASTE
PINNER
STANMORE
EDGWARE
FINCHLEY
PONDERS END
CHINGFORD
BUCKHURST
HAROLD WOOD
HARROW
WEMBLEY
HENDON
PALACE GATES
WOODFORD
FAIRLOP
GEORGE LANE
ROMFORD
GREENFORD
WILLESDEN
TOTTENHAM
SNARESBROOK
HORNCHURCH
UPMINSTER
EAST HORNDON
PITSEA
EALING
HACKNEY
ILFORD
SEVEN KINGS
LONDON TILBURY & SOUTHEND
Langdon Hill
HOUNSLOW
LONDON
STRATFORD
BARKING
DAGENHAM
RAINHAM
STANFORD LE HOPE
THAMES HAVEN
HAMMERSMITH
VICTORIA
WATERLOO
WOOLWICH
BECKTON
BELVEDERE
ERITH
PURFLEET
GRAYS
TILBURY DOCK
LOW STREET
RICHMOND
TWICKENHAM
CLAPHAM JUNC
GREENWICH
WELLING
BEXLEYHEATH
CRAYFORD
DARTFORD
NORTHFLEET
TILBURY
CLIFFE
S. E.
HAMPTON
KINGSTON
WIMBLEDON
TULSE HILL
NEW ELTHAM
SIDCUP
BEXLEY
GRAVESEND
ROCHESTER
STROO
SURBITON
MITCHAM
CROYDON
BROMLEY
MARY CRAY
ORPINGTON
CHISLEHURST
SOUTH EASTERN
SHANLEY
MEOPHAM
CARNINGHAM
CHATHAM
CUXTON
SOLE STR

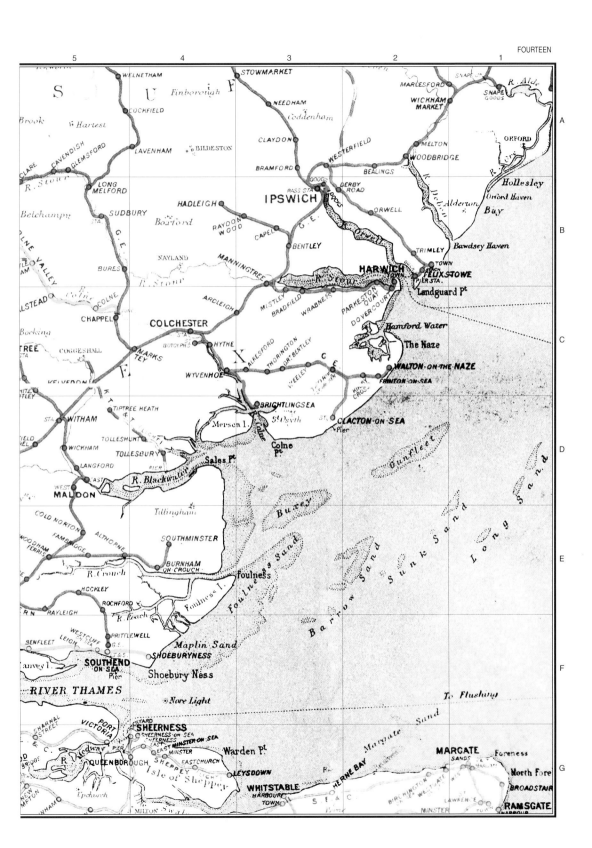

5   4   3   2   1

A

B

C

D

E

F

G

LLANRHYSTYD ROAD
LLANILAR
TRAWSCOED
R. Ystwyth
DEVIL'S BRIDGE
Cwmystwyth
PANTYDWR
ST HARMONS
LLANBISTER ROAD
LLANGUNLLO
*Fynydd
Abbey Cwm hir
R   A   D
Llanrhystyd
Ll. Euldwen bach
Mynydd bach
STRATA FLORIDA
Lan dd, fawr
Ll. Teifi
Birmingham Water Works
RHAYADER
PENYBONT
DOLAU
NEW RADNOR
O
Radnor Fo
Ll. Gynon
DOLDOWLOD
R. Wye
LLANDRINDOD WELLS
DO
G
I
D
TREGARON
NEWBRIDGE ON WYE
CAM.
BUILTH ROAD
L.&N.W. CAM.
JUNC.
BUILTH WELLS
Gladest
PONT LLANIO
L. Drygarn
R   E
CILMERY
GARTH
LLANGAMMARCH WELLS
CAM.
AEREDW
Painscastle
LLANGYBI
DERRY ORMOND
LAMPETER
Ffrorest yn Esgob
LLANWRTYD WELLS
ERWOOD
LLANYBYTHER
Nantymwyn
Mynydd Epynt
B
R
E
C
K
Pumpsaint
Cilycwm
R. Tywi
CYNGHORDY
BOUGHROOD
P. Wye
GLAS
THREE CO
STA
GIAU
LLANDOVERY
JUNC. STA.
Mynydd Eppynt torr.
TALGARTH
Bronllys
Bla
For
N
O
R
Llansawel
LLANWRDA
DEVYNOCK
ABERBRAN
CRADOC
BRECON
STA.
TREFEINON
CAMBRIAN
H
LLANGADOCK
R. Usk
Trecastle
TALYLLYN
JUNC. STA.
Ll. Safiddu
GLANRHYD
TALLEY ROAD
CRAY
NEATH & BRECON
R
GOLDEN GROVE
JUNC. BRIDGE
LLANDILO
Y Fan Brecheiniog
R. Tawe
Y Fan gihirach
PEN WYLLT
TALYBONT ON-USK
Bwlch
R. Usk
BRECON & MERTHYR
TALYBONT ON-USK
N.W.
DRYSLLWYN
FAIRFACH
OERWYDD ROAD
Fforest fawr
BRECKNOCK BEACONS
K
TURPANTAU
N
LLANARTHNE
LLANDEBIE
CARNAN
BRYN AMMAN
ABERCRAVE
PEN WYLLT
DOLYGAER
BRYNMAWR N.W.
BEAUFORT
CROSS HANDS
GLANAMMAN
ABERCRAVE
FONTSTICILL
NANTYBWCH
TREVIL
MAP
TUMBLE
TIRYDAIL
DOWLAIS CAE GURWEN
GWYS
YSTRADGYNLAIS
GLYN NEATH
RHYMNEY BRIDGE
PANT
EBBW VALE
CL
PANTYFFYNNON
AMMANFORD
GURNOS
YSTALYFERA
SEVEN SISTERS
CWMLLWYN
ABERMARCHOG
PONT SARN
MORLA
DOWLAIS
CEFN
TOE
VICTORIA
NAM
CL
CWM BLAWD
YNYS Y GEINON JUNC.
R. Ischaw
DOLAIN
THEDEGAR
ORE
GW
CEFN
RHYMNEY
EB
R. Twrch
NEATH & BRECON
CRYNANT
GREAT WESTERN
COLBREN JUNC.
GLYN NEATH
MERTHYR
CWM
EARCOED
TIR PHIL
NEW TREDEGAR
BLEWELTY
MILLS
PONTARDULAIS
G.W. L.&N.W.
PONTARDAWE
MIDLAND
NEATH & BRECON
RESOLVEN
HIRWAIN G.W.
LLWYDCOED MILL
ABER CWM
ABERCANAID
PENYR BACH
PENTRE YBANN
GOER NANT
ERITH HEN
BARGOED
CRU
LLAN GENNECH SGAFEN
BYNEA
GURN EINON
CILFREW
NEATH ABBEY
AVON
BLAENWYNFI
ABERDYLAIS
BLAEN PHONCO
ABERDARE
ABER AMAN
CWMBACH
ABER
MARDY
TREAUBERY
MOUNTAIN ASH
PENYRHEOL
NANT GARW
FENWYRHIW
QUAKERS
PENGAM
BLACK WOOD
MOPRISTON
FLAG MARL
LLANSAMLET
NEATH
JUNC
DYNEVOR
NEATH
NEW CASTLE
CWM AVON
MAERDY
YSTRADFELLTE DALE
ASHM WRTH
HAFOD
ABERCWM
HENGOED
TREGG
MAEL
BW
OUGHOR AWDD
GOWERTON
COCKETT
HIGH ST RUTLAND
BRITON FERRY
NEATH JUNC
PONT RHYDYFEN
CYMMER
CAERAU
NANTY FFYLON
NANTYMOEL
YSTRAD
LLWYNYPIA
LINAS
ABER PORTH
BRACHI
CLYDACH
NINE MIL
LLAN
DUNVANT
KILLAY
MUMBLES ROAD
SWANSEA
ABERAVON SEA SIDE
MASS GRAIG
CWM AVON R.&S.B.
PORT TALBOT
PONT CAW
PONTY RHYLL
PEN YR FORTH
PONTY CYMMER
COSMORE VALE
PONTY PRIDD
FOREST MYNACH
HNO
CAW
BRACAN
LLAN HENITH
TAFFS WELL
MUMBLES
Swansea Bay
PORT TALBOT
MARGAM
DOCKS
SEA SIDE
TR. EDYFHIEW GARTH
LLANGONWYD
LLETTY BRONGU
BETW
LLANGEINOR
LLANFIHON
TREFFR ST
BLACK MILL
THE VILLAGE
CAERPHILLY
RHY
G
MUMBLES Hd
Caswell B.
Lawich
R.
GREAT
MENFIG HY
TONDU
BRYNMENYN LLANHARAN
CAR
WESTERN
TAFFS WELL

1   2   3   4   5

A

FANAU
TOWYN
ABERDOVEY
R. Dovey
Afon Dysy
TAL-Y-LLYN
DOLGOCH
BRYNGLAS
PANDYVRCNEN
ABERGYNOLWYN
BRACH GOCH
CRIS
CORRIS
CEMMES ROAD
LLWYNGWERN
FFRIDD GATE
CEMMES
MACHYNLLETH
GLANDOVEY
CAMBRIAN
LLANBRYNMAIR
TALERDDIG
CARNO
CERIST GARW CEILIOG
CWM LINE
COED ULO
M O N T G O M
CAEREINION GATE
HENIARTH GATE
CYFRONYDD
CASTLE CAERENION
SYLFAEN FARM
GOLFA
RAVEN SQUARE
SEVEN STARS
Trwynon
FORDEN
MONTGOMERY

YNYS LAS
Pen Daren
PONTDOLGOCH
CAERSWS
TREWITHAN
RED HOUSE
TREFEGLWYS
GARTH ROAD
VANI
CHRIST
MOAT LANE JUNC
SCAFELL GOONS
R. Severn
NEWTOWN
ABERMULE
KERRY
Kerry Hill

B

BORTH
STWYTH
CAMBRIAN
LLANFIHANGEL
BOW STREET
PLINLIMMON
R. Severn
R. Tre
CAMBRIAN
DOLWEN
LLANDINAM
LLANIDLOES
TYLWCH
Pegwyn fawr
Llanbadarn Fynydd

C

LLANRHYSTYD ROAD
CAPEL BANGOR
NANTYRONEN
ABERFFRWD
VALE OF RHEIDOL
LLANBADARN
DEVIL'S BRIDGE
Ponterwyd
Llangurig
LLANILAR
TRAWSCOED
Cwmystwyth
R. Ystwyth
Lan du fawr
Ll. Teifi
R
PANTYDWR
ST HARMONS
Abbey Cwm-hir
A
LLANBISTER ROAD
LLANGUNLLO
D
Llanrhystyd
H. Eiddwen bach
Mynydd bach
G
STRATA FLORIDA
A. Teifi
Ll. Gynon
Birmingham Water Works
RHAYADER
PENYBONT
DOLAU
O
Radnor Fo
NEW RADNOR

D

on
D
I
D
Carn gron
TREGARON
PONT LLANIO
B. Drygarn
DOLGOWLOD
R. Wye
NEWBRIDGE ON WYE
CAM
LLANDRINDOD WELLS
DO
Glades

E

LLANGYBI
DERRY ORMOND
LAMPETER
MANCHESTER & MILFORD
Fforest yr Esgob
LLANYBYTHER
Nantymwyn
Ll. Teivy
LONDON & NORTH WESTERN
LLANWRTYD WELLS
LLANGAMMARCH WELLS
GARTH
CILMERY
BUILTH ROAD
L.&N.W. CAM.
BUILTH WELLS
JUNC
ABEREDW
ERWOOD
B
R
E
C
K
Mynydd Epynt
Painscastle

F

Llansawel
Pumpsaint
UGIAU
Cilycwm
R. Towy
CYNGHORDY
LLANDOVERY
JUNC STA
LLANWRDA
LLANGADOCK
GLANRHYD
TALLEY ROAD
Mynydd Bwlch y groes
VALE OF TOWY
G.W. & L&N.W. JCT.
R. Usk
Trecastle
DEVYNOCK
ABERBRAN
CRACIO
BRECON
TREFEINON
TALGARTH
CAMBRIAN
THREE CO
GLAS L & N W
P. Wye
BOUGHROOD
Bronllys
Bla
For
TALYLLYN
Ll. Safaddu
R
O
R
T
H
F
N
E

G

GOLDEN GROVE
DRYSLLWYN
(LLANARTHNE)
N. W.
LLANDILO BRIDGE JUNC
FAIRFACH
LLANDILO
DERWYDD ROAD
Y Fan Brecheiniog
Y Fan
gihirach
CRAY
NEATH & BRECON
BRECKNOCK BEACONS
TALYBONT ON USK
Bwlch
E. Usk
BRECON & MERTHYR
CROSS HANDS
GLANAMMAN
CARNAN
LLANDEBIE
BRYN AMMAN
R. Tawe
PENWYLLT
Forest fawr
Neath
TURPANTAU
DOLYGAER
NANTYBWO
RH
BRYNMAWR
BEAUFORT
TREVIL L.N.W.
N.W.
TIRYDAIL
ABERCRAVE
M. O.
FONTSTICILL

5   4   3   2   1

WELSHPOOL

SNAILBEACH (Gauge 2'4")
SNAILBEACH MINE
CROWSNEST MINE

MINSTERLEY
PONTESBURY
LEA LE R?
CONDOVER

DORRINGTON
CRESSAGE
BUILDWAS
IRON BRIDGE
COALBROOKDALE
HORSEHAY
LIGHTMOOR
BRICHLEY
MADELEY/SALOP
MADELEY MARKET
L & NW
COALPORT
G.W.
ALBRIGHTON
CODSALL
BUSHBURY
DUNSTALL PARK

Churbury
Snsuperstones
Caer Caradoc

SHREWSBURY & HEREFORD
G.W. & L.N.W. JOINT

LEEBOTWOOD
CHURCH STRETTON
PRESTHOPE
LONGVILLE
MUCH WENLOCK
LINLEY
BRIDGNORTH
EARDINGTON
HAMPTON LOADE
HIGHLEY
ARLEY

Morville
Worfield
Wombourne
Enville

WOLVERHAMPTON
MONMORE GRE
PRIES
ETTINGHALL R? S. BILS

STOURBRIDGE
JUNC STA
HAGLEY
CHURCHILL
KIDDERMINST

Church Stoke
LYDHAM HEATH
BISHOPS CASTLE
EATON
PLOWDEN
HORDERLEY
STRETFORD BRIDGE STA
STRETFORD BRIDGE
BISHOPS CASTLE
MARSH BROOK
MARSH FARM
HARTON ROAD
RUSHBURY
CAER CARADOC

GREAT WESTERN

Brown Clee
Burwarton
Kinlet

CRAVEN ARMS & STOKESAY
BROOME
ONIBURY
BROMFIELD
MIDDLETON
BITTERLEY
CLEE HILL

Titterstone Clee

HOPTON HEATH
BUCKNELL
Leintwardine
LUDLOW
Bringewood Chase

KNUCHLAS
KNIGHTON
L. & N.W.

WYRE FOREST
CLEOBURY MORTIMER
NEEN SOLLARS
BEWDLEY
STOURPORT
HARTLEBURY

Rock
Gr! Witley

DROITWICH STA.

Wigmore
Norton
R. Lugg

WOOFFERTON
TENBURY
EASTON COURT
NEWNHAM BRIDGE

R. Teme
Clifton
Hallows

PRESTEIGN
KINGSLAND
BERRINGTON & EYE

PEMBRIDGE
TITLEY
LYHIR
STANNER
KINGTON GRT WESTERN
LYONSHALL

LEOMINSTER JUNC
FORD BRIDGE
STEENS BRIDGE
FENCOTE
ROWDEN MILL
BROMYARD
KNIGHTWICK
SUCKLEY
LEIGH COURT
BRANSFORD ROAD
G.W.

WORCESTER
FOREGATE STR
HENWICK
SHRUB HILL
MID GOODS
FERNHILL HEATH

ALMELEY
WEOBLEY
DINMORE
Stoke Lacy

NORTON JUNC
WADBOROUGH

EARDISLEY
WHITNEY ON THE WYE
CLIFFORD
KINNERSLEY JUNC
WESTBROOK
MOORHAMPTON
CREDENHILL
MIDLAND
MORETON ON LUGG
SHELWICK JUNC
WITHINGTON
STOKE EDITH
COLWALL
MALVERN LINK
GRT MALVERN
MALVERN WELLS
DEFFORD
Cradley
Malvern Hills

HAY
JUNC STA
DORSTONE
G.W.
Golden Valley
FETERCHURCH
VOWCHURCH

HEREFORD
MOORFIELDS
BARTON GOODS
BARRS COURT JUNC
STA (BARTON)
BARRS COURT S. JN
ROTHERWAS JUNC
RED HILL JUNC
L.N.W.

BARTON
ASHPERTON
GREAT WESTERN
LEDBURY
Eastnor
UPTON ON SEVERN
RIPPLE
TEWKESBURY

R. Wye
HOLME LACY
TRAM INN
Kingstone
Much Marcle

BACTON
ABBEYDORE
ST DEVEREUX
FAWLEY
DYMOCK
Staunton
Tirley
R. Severn

Black Mountain
Llanthony
Hoarwithy

GREAT WESTERN
PONTRILAS STA JUNC

NEWENT
ROSS G.W.
MITCHELDEAN ROAD
May Hill
BARBERS BRIDGE
CHURCHDOWN

CHE
GLOUCESTER

FANDY
Grosmont
St Weonards
Skenfrith

LLANVIHANGEL
Sugar Loaf

Goodrich Castle
KERNE BRIDGE
LYDBROOK JUNC
SYMONDS YAT
CINDERFORD
GRANGE COURT
OAKLE STREET
LONGHOPE

ABERGAVENNY
GOVILON
MONMOUTH
ROSS

SPEECH
NEWNHAM
BILSON GDS

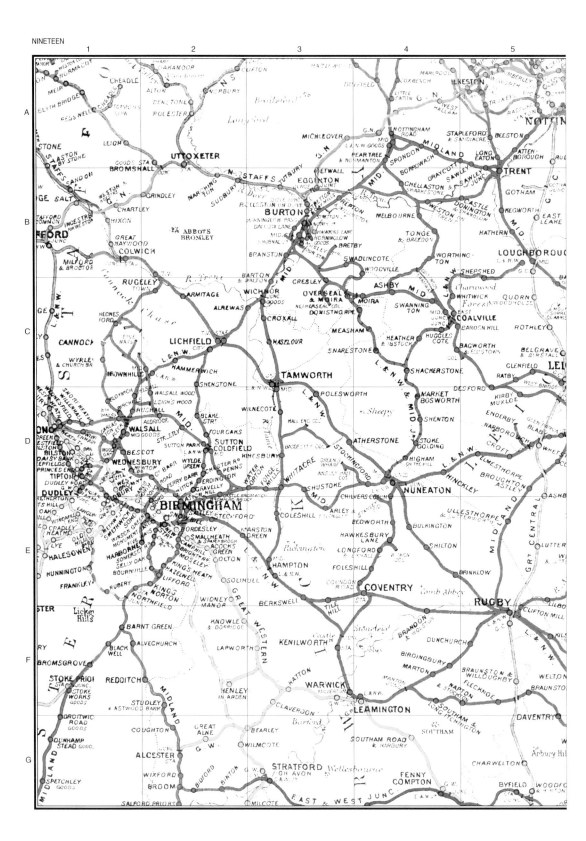

5   4   3   2   1

A

B

C

D

E

F

G

SLOWGH
NEWTON
BINGHAM
BOTTESFORD
ELTON
HOUGHAM
Bennington
HONACTON
ANCASTER
ASWARBY
HELPRINGHAM
WHINSTEAD
GHAM
G.N.
RADCLIFFE
BARKSTONE
Belton
GRANTHAM
EDWALTON
BARNSTONE
REDMILE
CANAL YARD STA
BILLINGBORO
CONINGTON ROAD
PLUMTREE
DUKE OF RUTLAND'S SIDG
FOLKINGHAM
MIDLAND
M.S.R CH
WIDMERPOOL
HARBY & STATHERN
STAVELEY & OAKS COS SID
STAVELEY & REDWOOD
DENTON SID
GREAT PONTON
RIPPINGALE
COSRENTON
SPALDING
UPPER BROUGHTON
LONG CLAWSON
WALTHAM ON THE WOLD
Woolsthorpe
CORBY
MORTON ROAD
PINCHBECK
MID GOODS
STA
OLD DALBY
MID SCALFORD
SAXBY
EDMONDTHORPE
SOUTH WITHAM
Grimsthorpe Park
Elenham
EASTGATE
WEST
JOINT
GRIMSTON
HOLWELL
ASFORDI
FRISBY
GR DALBY
WHISSENDINE
MID
BOURNE
TWENTY
COUNTER DRAIN
NORTH DROVE
ARROW- ON SOAR & QUORN
MELTON MOWBRAY
CASTLE BYTHAM
LITTLE BYTHAM
THURLBY
G.N.
LITTLEWORTH
SILEBY
BROOKSBY
REARSBY
ASHWELL
COTTESMORE RUTRE MINES
ESSENDINE
BRACEBORO SPA
MARKET DEEPING
CROWLA
SYSTON
JOHN O GAUNT
OAKHAM
RYHALL
TALLINGTON
ST JAMES DEEPING
FR
CESTER
HUMBERSTONE
THURNBY & SCRAPTOFT
MARFIELD JUNCS
TILTON
STAMFORD
PEAKIRK
MID & G.
GN. STA
MID GOODS
Billesdon
MANTON
LUFFENHAM STA
KETTON
UFFINGTON
BARNACK
WERRINGTON JUNC
EYE GREEN
EAST NORTON
MORCOTT
WAVERLEY
BARNACK UFFORD BRIDGE
HELPSTON
MID
PETERBORO
WIGSTON
UPPINGHAM
SEATON
KINGSCLIFFE
WANSFO ROAD
WANSFORD
WALTON
G.N. GOODS
FLETTON
WHITT
GREAT GLEN
HALLATON
HARRINGWORTH
GRETTON
NASSINGTON
CASTOR
ELTON
OVERTON
STONE
KIBWORTH
MEDBOURNE
ROCKINGHAM
Fotheringhay Cas
L. & N.W.
YAXLEY & FARCET
EAG LANGTN
ASHLEY
WELDON CORBY
Brigstock
OUNDLE
Stibbin
Y MAGNA
MARKET HARBOROUGH
DESBOROUGH
GEDDINGTON
BARNWELL
Sawtry &c
ST MARY
THEDDINGWORTH
GT. BOWDEN
ROTHWELL
GLENDON JUNC
CRANFORD
TWYWELL
THORPE
HOLME
G.N. & G.
CLIFTON & OXENDEN
GLENDON & RUSHTON
GREAT NORTHERN
WORTH
ELFORD
KELMARSH
THRAPSTON
ABBOTS RIPTON
Alconbury
YELVERTOFT & STANFORD PARK
Naseby
KETTERING STA
RAUNDS
HUNTING
G
URNE
LAMPORT
LOGDINGTON
ISHAM
RINGSTEAD & ADDINGTON
Spaldwick
HUNTINGDON
SBY &
BRIXWORTH
FINEDON
H FERRERS
HIGHAM FERRERS
MIDLAND
ST NEOTS
W. Haddon
SPRATTON
DITCHFORD
RUSHDEN
KIMBOLTON LONG STOW
BUCKDEN
OFFORD
LONG BUCKBY
ALTHORP PARK
PITSFORD & BRAMPTON
WELLINGBOROUGH
IRCHESTER
OAKLEY
GRAFHAM
Eston
L. & N.W.
MIDLAND
EEDON
NORTHAMPTON
CASTLE STA MID
CASTLE ASHBY & EARLS BARTON
SHARNBROOK
ST NEOTS
Eaton Socon
OLD N.
BILLING
PIDDINGTON
HARROLD
Milton Ernest
R. Nene
BLISWORTH
SALCEY FOREST GOODS
OLNEY
TURVEY
WILLINGTON
BLUNHAM
TEMPSFORD
ROADE
OAKLEY

HEADINGS/REGION LABELS (large faint lettering across map):
S MIDLAND · W NOTTS · LEICESTER · E FOREST · RUTLAND · LINCOLNSHIRE · NORTHAMPTON · HUNTING

1 2 3 4 5

Brancaster Roads

A BOSTON Gore Py HOLKHAM WELL
Chandlin BURNHAM MARKET

THE HUNSTANTON Bircham DOCKING STANHOE B
KIRTON WASH HEACHAM SEDGEFORD WALSINGHAM THUR

ALGARKIRK SNETTISHAM Syderstone

B SURFLEET DERSINGHAM RAYNHAM PARK FAKENHAM
WESTON MOULTON WHAPLODE HOLBEACH FLEET GEDNEY WOLFERTON EAST RUDHAM RYBURGH
KING SUTTON Sandringham MID & GN JOINT
MID. & G N JOINT SUTTON BRIDGE NORTH WOOTTON Castle Rising GRT. NORTHERN JOINT West Raynham
COWBIT YDD V'ALPOLE TERRINGTON CLENCHWARTON LYNN HILLINGTON MASSINGHAM COUNTY SC
STA DOCKS MIDLAND & GRT NORTHERN JOINT GRIMSTON RD NORTH ELM

C FERRY SOUTHERY GAYTON ROAD EAST WINCH LITCHAM
HARBOUR HARDWICK ROAD GOODS MIDDLETON N Castle Acre R
NARBOROUGH GREAT EASTERN
POSTLAND MAGDALEN ROAD R. Nar TRANSHAM WENDLING
LAND FRENCH DROVE WISBECH MIDDLE DROVE STOW SWAFFHAM DUNHAM STA
WISBECH ST MARY MEETH ROAD Fincham HOLME HALE Shipdham
G.N. JOINT MURROW EMNETH BOXES BR ECTFIELD BASIN DOWNHAM HOLME HALE
THORNEY WRYDE GUYHIRNE COLDHAM OUTWELL VILLAGE OUTWELL DENVER STOKE FERRY Gooderstone WATTON

D GRASSMOOR JUNC G ABBEY RYSTON Stoke R. R. Wissey
OUGH GREAT EASTERN MARCH HILGAY Southery STOW BEDON
TLESEA STONEA Mattorld Mundford WRETHAM & HOCKHAM
BENWICK GOODS WIMBLINGTON MANEA LITTLEPORT Little Ouse R. GRT EAS
RY'S CHATTERIS BLACK BANK LAKENHEATH BRANDON Roudham
RAMSEY CHETTISHAM BURNT FEN THETFORD

E WARBOYS Elveden BARNHAM Easton
SOMERSHAM SUTTON STA ELY Eriswell
St IVES EARITH BRIDGE HADDENHAM Lackford r. INGHAM IXWO
F MANCHESTER BLUNTISHAM WILBURTON STRETHAM ISLEHAM MILDENHALL
SWAVESEY SOHAM FORDHAM KENNET HIGHAM SAXHAM G.E. BURY ST EDMUNDS EAST GATE THURSTO
LONG STANTON OAKINGTON WATERBEACH SWAFFHAM PRIOR BURWELL NEWMARKET Barrow Ickworth
Papworth HISTON BOTTISHAM & LODE WELNETHAM
CAXTON BARNWELL QUY
G CAMBRIDGE DULLINGHAM Ludgate

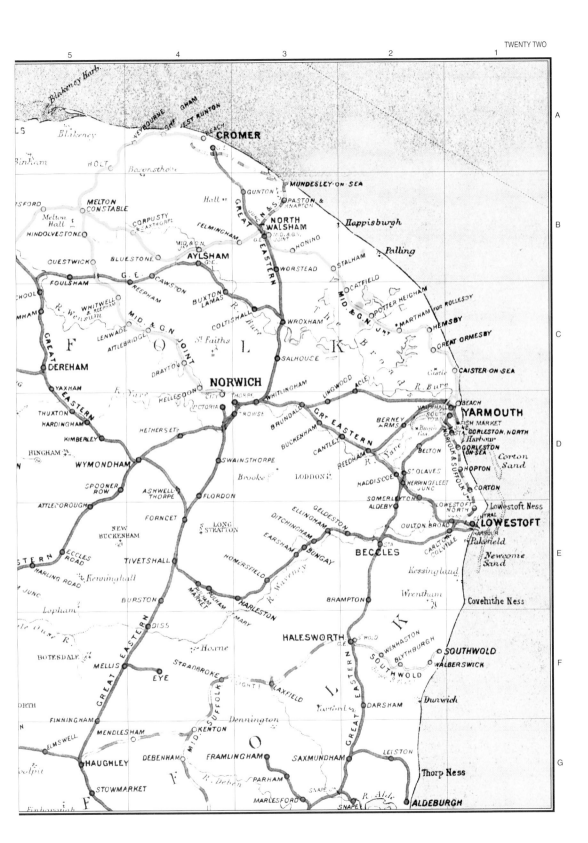

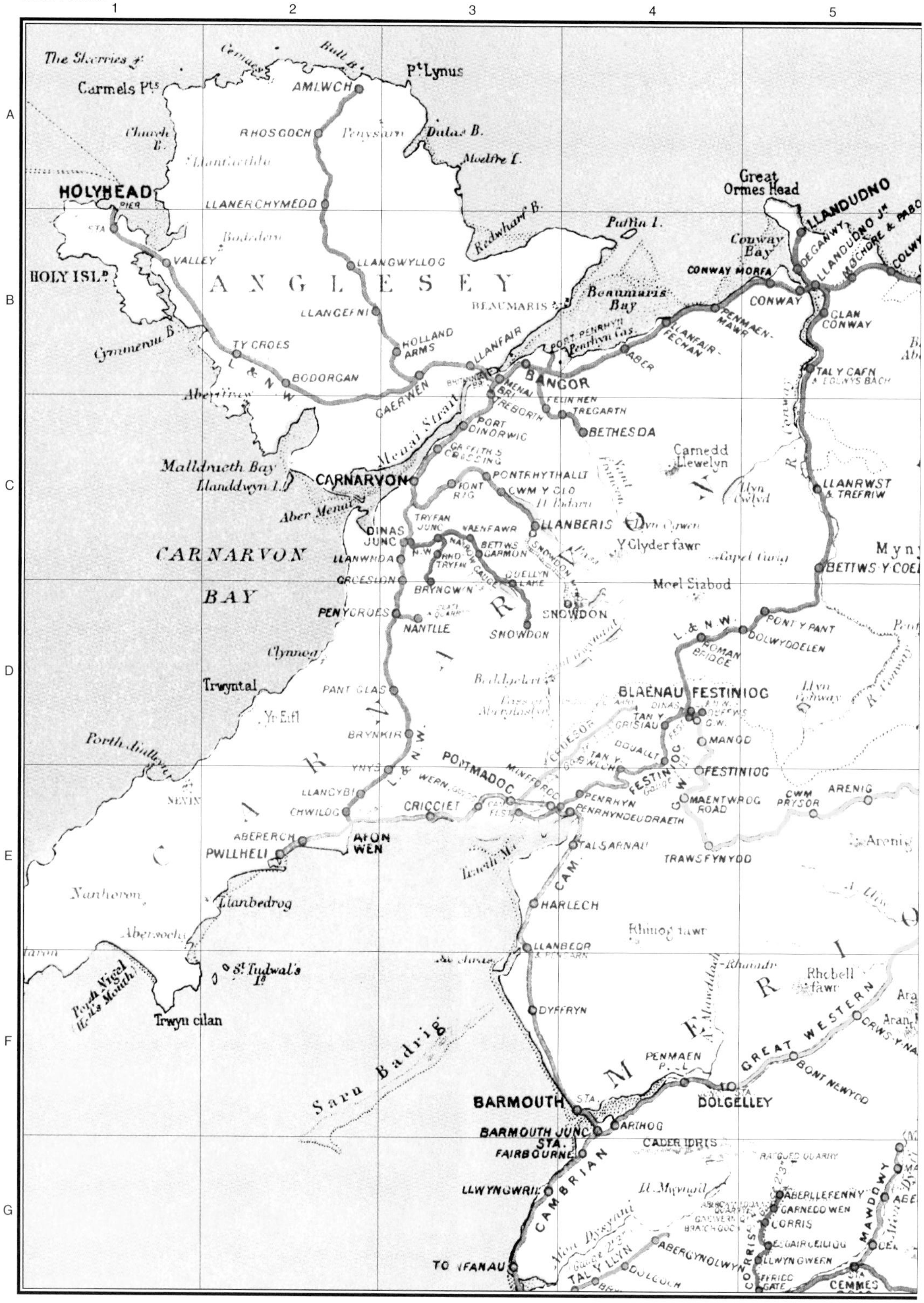
The Skerries
Carmels Pts
Church B.
HOLYHEAD
PIER
STA
HOLY ISLD
VALLEY
Cymmeran B.
TY CROES
L & N W
BODORGAN
Aberffraw
Malldraeth Bay
Llanddwyn I.
CARNARVON
BAY
Bull B.
Pt Lynus
AMLWCH
RHOSGOCH
Penysarn
Dulas B.
Moelfre I.
LLANERCHYMEDD
LLANGWYLLOG
ANGLESEY
LLANGEFNI
HOLLAND ARMS
GAERWEN
LLANFAIR
BEAUMARIS
Beaumaris Bay
Puffin I.
Redwharf B.
Menai Strait
MENAI BRI.
TREBORTH
BANGOR
PORT PENRHYN
Penrhyn Cas.
ABER
LLANFAIR-FECHAN
PENMAEN-MAWR
CONWAY MORFA
CONWAY
Conway Bay
Great Ormes Head
LLANDUDNO
DEGANWY
LLANDUDNO JN
MOCHDRE & PABO
COLWYN
GLAN CONWAY
TAL Y CAFN & EGLWYS BACH
R. Conway
LLANRWST & TREFRIW
BETTWS-Y-COED
FELIN HEN
TREGARTH
BETHESDA
Carnedd Llewelyn
PORT DINORWIC
GRIFFITH'S CROSSING
PONTRHYTHALLT
PONT RUG
CWM Y GLO
LLANBERIS
Y Glyder fawr
Capel Curig
Moel Siabod
DINAS JUNC
TRYFAN JUNC
WAENFAWR
BETTWS GARMON
LLANWNDA
GROESLON
BRYNGWYN
QUELLYN LAKE
SNOWDON
PENYGROES
NANTLLE
Clynnog
Trwyntal
Yr Eifl
Porth dinllaen
NEVIN
Beddgelert
PANT GLAS
BRYNKIR
YNYS
LLANGYBI
CHWILOG
ABERERCH
PWLLHELI
AFON WEN
Llanbedrog
Nanhoron
Abersoch
Porth Nigel
Hell's Mouth
St Tudwal's Is
Trwyn cilan
CRICCIETH
PORTMADOC
MINFFORDD
PENRHYN
PENRHYNDEUDRAETH
TALSARNAU
HARLECH
LLANBEDR & PENSARN
DYFFRYN
Sarn Badrig
BARMOUTH
BARMOUTH JUNC STA.
FAIRBOURNE
ARTHOG
LLWYNGWRIL
CAMBRIAN
TONFANAU
TAL Y LLYN
DOLGOCH
ABERGYNOLWYN
L. & N. W.
PONT Y PANT
DOLWYDDELEN
ROMAN BRIDGE
BLAENAU FESTINIOG
TAN Y GRISIAU
DUFFWS
G.W.
MANOD
DDUALLT
TAN Y BWLCH
FESTINIOG
MAENTWROG ROAD
TRAWSFYNYDD
CWM PRYSOR
ARENIG
Llyn Arenig
Rhinog fawr
Rhobell fawr
GREAT WESTERN
DRWS-Y-NANT
BONT NEWYDD
PENMAEN POOL
DOLGELLEY
CADER IDRIS
ABERLLEFENNY
CORRIS
MAWDDWY
CEMMES
1
2
3
4
5
A
B
C
D
E
F
G

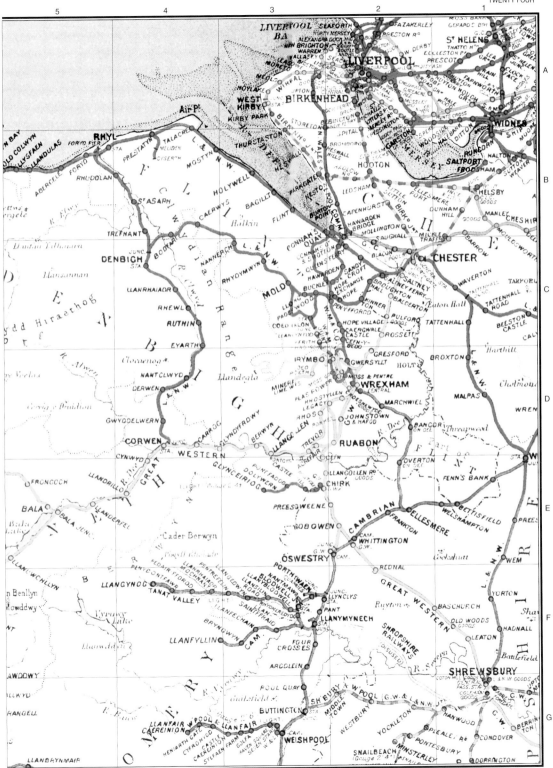

1   2   3   4   5

A

B

C

D

E

F

G

LIVERPOOL
BIRKENHEAD
MANCHESTER
WARRINGTON
WIDNES
RUNCORN
HOOTON
CHESTER
NORTHWICH
KNUTSFORD
CONGLETON
SANDBACH
CREWE
NANTWICH
WREXHAM
RUABON
LLANGOLLEN
CHIRK
OSWESTRY
WHITCHURCH
MARKET DRAYTON
ELLESMERE
LLANYMYNECH
SHREWSBURY
WELLINGTON
NEWCASTLE
HANLEY
ST HELENS
AINTREE
WATERLOO
BIRKENHEAD
MOLD
TARPORLEY
MALPAS
WRENBURY
PREES
WEM
CAMBRIAN
GREAT WESTERN
L. & N.W.
G.W.
N. STAFFS
CHESHIRE LINES

5   4   3   2   1

PENISTONE
GREENFIELD
FRIEZLAND
MOSSLEY
MICKLEHURST
DIGLEY & MILLBROOK
STALYBRIDGE
DUKINFIELD
HADFIELD
GLOSSOP
MOTTRAM
HYDE
WOODLE
BREDBURY
GREAT CENTRAL
CROWDEN
WOODHEAD
BIRDWELL & HOYLAND
CHAPELTOWN
ECCLESFIELD
HARGATE
ROTHERHAM ROAD
SWINTON
MEXBORO
CONISBORO
DENABY
WATH
WOMBWELL
BARNSLEY
DEARFIELD
SPROTBORO

PORT
MARPLE
HAYFIELD
THE PEAK
BIRCHVALE
NEW MILLS
EDALE
Ashopton
DISLEY
BOLLINGTON
CHAPEL EN LE FRITH
WHALEY BRIDGE
DOVE HOLES
PEAK FOREST
HOPE
BAMFORD
HATHERSAGE
GRINDLEFORD
NEEPSEND
SHEFFIELD
HEELEY
DORE
KILLAMARSH
BEIGHTON
WOODHOUSE MILL
ROTHERHAM
LAUGHTON
KIVETON PARK
SHIRCOAKS
DRONFIELD
SPINKHILL
DECKINGTON
BARLBRO
STAVELEY
CRESWELL
ELMTON
WHITWELL
Welbeck Park

ECCLESFIELD
BUXTON
HIGHER BUXTON
LADMANLOW GOODS
HARPUR HILL
HINDLOW
TIDESWELL
MILLERS DALE
MONSAL DALE
LONGSTONE
HASSOP
BAKEWELL
CHATSWORTH
Baslow
CHESTERFIELD
SHEEPBRIDGE
BRAMPTON
CALOW
GRASSMOOR
HASLAND GOODS
STAVELEY
BOLSOVER
LANGWITH
WARSOP
SHIREBROOK
MANSFIELD WOODHOUSE
MANSFIELD

NORTH RODE
BOSLEY
RUSHTON
Lud's Church
TONGNOR
The Roaches
Mee brook
HARTINGTON
HULME END
WINSTER
MATLOCK
BATH
ROWSLEY
HADDON HALL
DARLEY DALE
CLAY CROSS
TRETTON
DOE LEA
TIBSHELF
WHITEBORO
SKEGBY
SUTTON JUNC.
SUTTON
KIRKBY-IN-ASHFIELD
MANSFIELD

LEEK
WALL GRANGE
CHEDDLETON
STOCKTON BROOK
MILTON
BUCKNALL
CONSALL
CALDON LOW
WATERHOUSES
WEAVER HILLS
FROGHALL
OAKAMOOR
HARTINGTON
ALSOP
TISSINGTON
FENNY BENTLEY
THORPE CLOUD
ASHBOURNE
WIRKSWORTH
CROMFORD
STEEPLE HOUSE
WHATSTANDWELL
WINGFIELD
ALFRETON
PINXTON
PYE BRIDGE
CODNOR PARK
AMBERGATE
RIPLEY
CODNOR
EASTWOOD
ANNESLEY
NEWSTEAD
LINBY
HUCKNALL
BUTLER'S HILL

CHEADLE
ALTON
DENSTONE
ROCESTER
CLIFTON
NORBURY
DUFFIELD
BELPER
DENBY
HEANOR
KIRK LANGLEY
ILKESTON
KIMBERLEY
BASFORD
NOTTING
CHEADLE
TOTMONS LOW
BLYTHE BRIDGE
Bentley
Longford
DERBY
MICKLEOVER
NOTTINGHAM ROAD
STAPLEFORD & SANDIACRE
BEESTON
MIDLAND
LONG EATON
ATTENBOROUGH

STONE
ASTON-BY-STONE
SANDON
STAFFORD
INGESTRE
SALT
GRINDLEY
UTTOXETER
BROMSHALL
MARCHINGTON
SUDBURY
STAFFS
TUTBURY
EGGINTON JUNC.
ETWALL
PEAR TREE & NORMANTON
SPONDON
BORROWASH
DRAYCOTT
SAWLEY
TRENT
GOTHAM
CHELLASTON & SWARKESTONE
CASTLE DONINGTON & SHARDLOW
KEGWORTH
EAST LEAKE

STAFFORD
HIXON
COLWICH
CHARTLEY
ABBOTS BROMLEY
GREAT HAYWOOD
BRANSTON
BURTON
HORNINGLOW
DALLOW LANE
REPTON
STRETTON
SWADLINCOTE
MELBOURNE
WESTON ON TRENT
TONGE & BREEDON
HATHERN
WORTHINGTON
LOUGHBOROUGH

RUGELEY TOWN
ARMITAGE
HEDNESFORD
FIVE WAYS
ALREWAS
WICHNOR JUNC.
BARTON & WALTON
CRESLEY
WOODVILLE
ASHBY
SHEPSHED
CHARNWOOD FOREST
WHITWICK
WOODHOUSE
QUORN
CANNOCK CHASE
LICHFIELD
CROXALL
HASELOUR
MEASHAM
OVERSEAL & MOIRA
MOIRA
DONISTHORPE
SWANNINGTON
HEATHER
HUGGLESCOTE
COALVILLE
BARDON HILL
ROTHLEY
EAST JUNC.
MOUNT SORREL QUARRIES

A
B
C
D
E
F
G

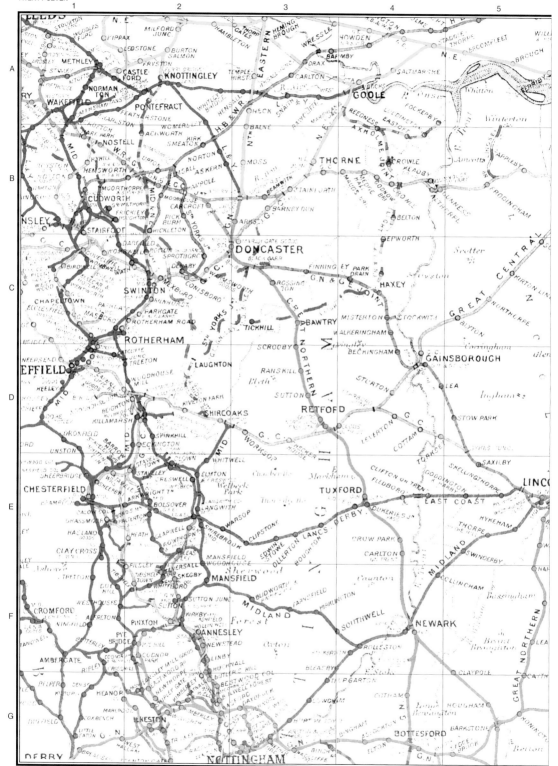

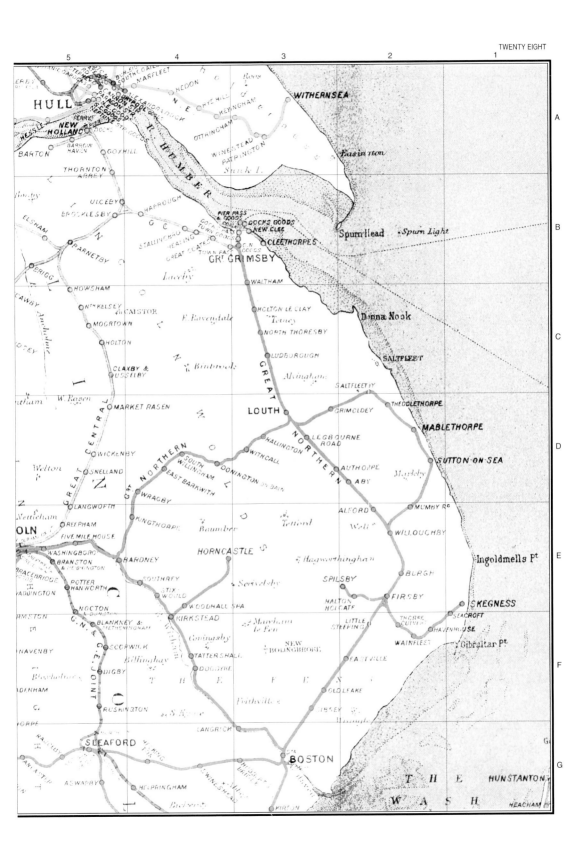

5   4   3   2   1

A
B
C
D
E
F
G

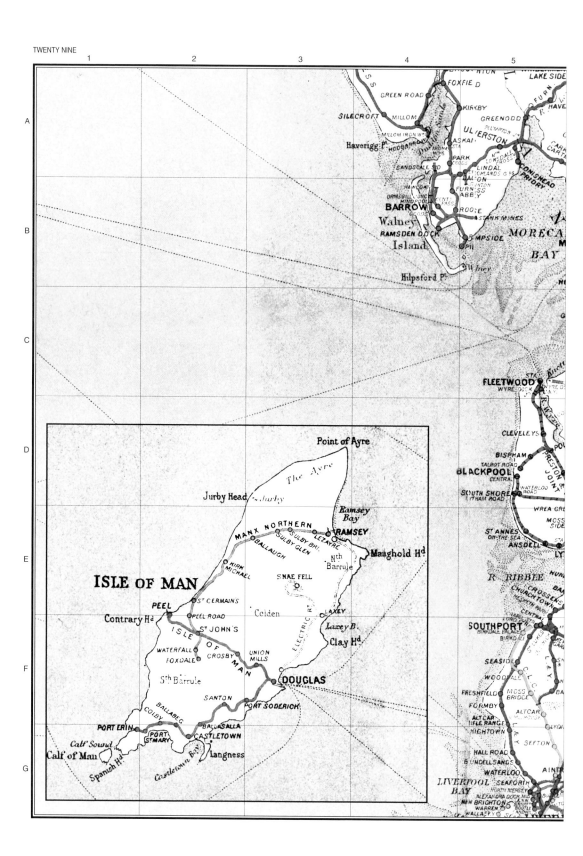

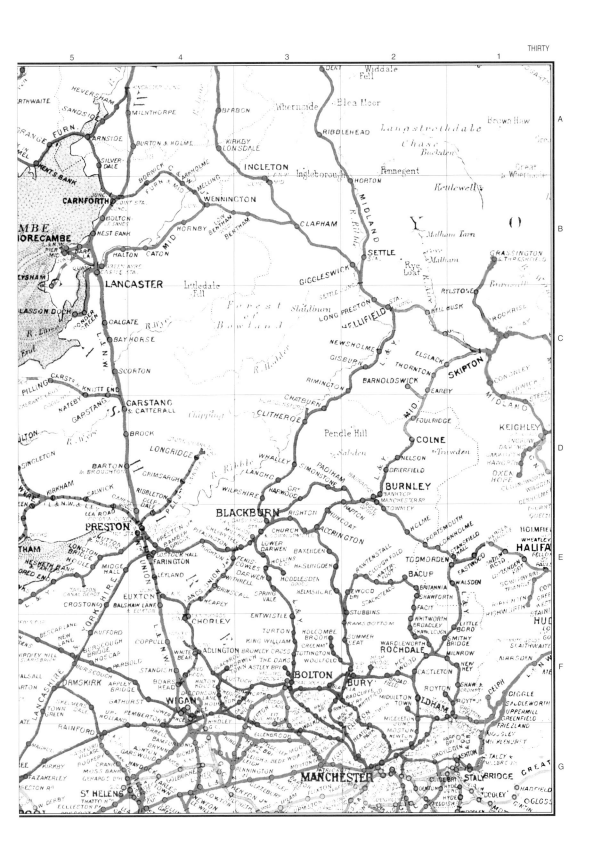

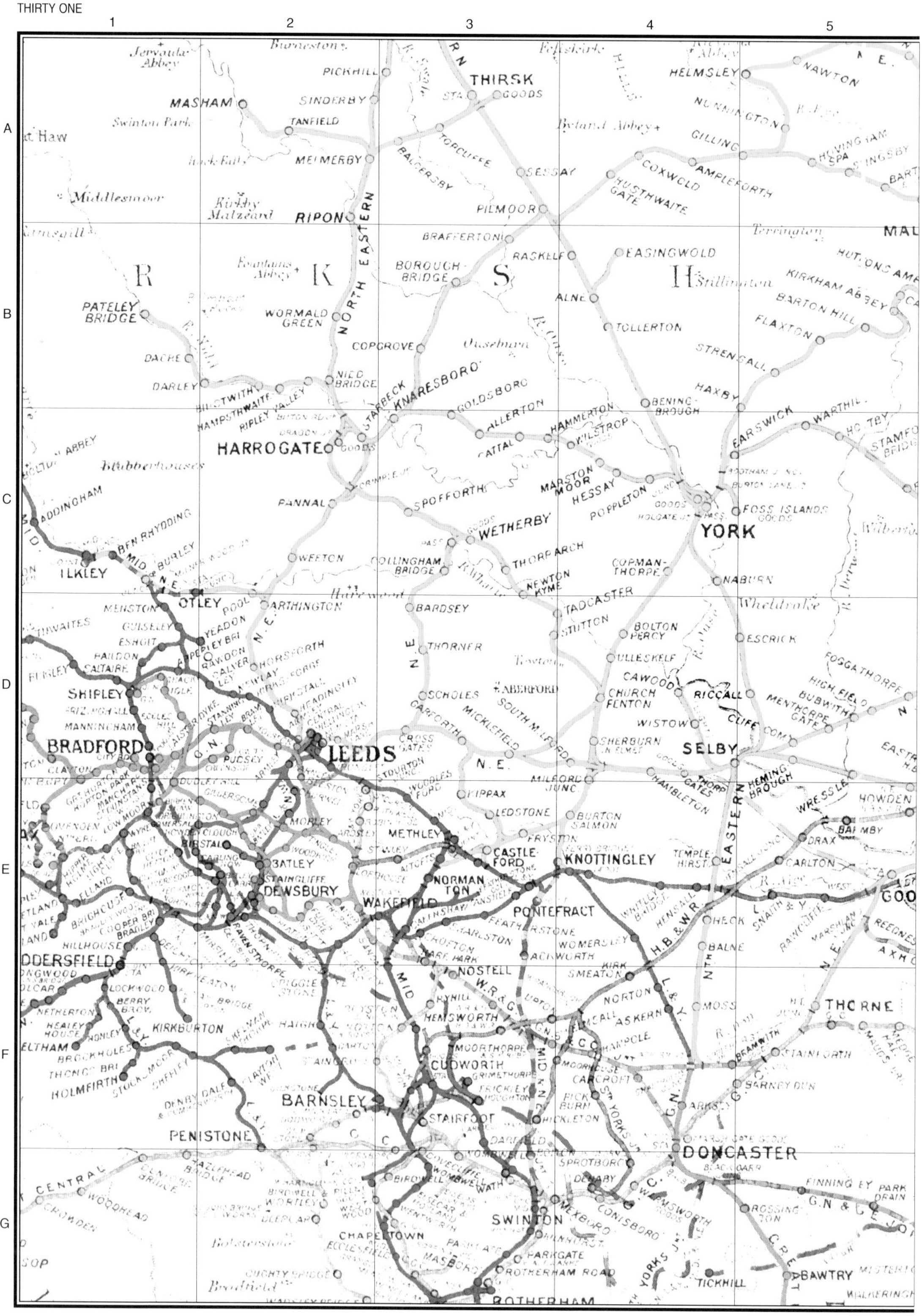
1
2
3
4
5
A
B
C
D
E
F
G
Jervaulx Abbey
MASHAM
Swinton Park
PICKHILL
SINDERBY
TANFIELD
MELMERBY
Kirkby Malzeard
Middlesmoor
RIPON
NORTH EASTERN
THIRSK
GOODS
TORCLIFFE
BALDERSBY
SESSAY
PILMOOR
Byland Abbey
HELMSLEY
NAWTON
NUNNINGTON
GILLING
AMPLEFORTH
COXWOLD
HUSTHWAITE GATE
HOVINGHAM SPA
SLINGSBY
BRAFFERTON
RASKELF
EASINGWOLD
Fountains Abbey
R
K
S
H
BOROUGH-BRIDGE
PATELEY BRIDGE
WORMALD GREEN
ALNE
TOLLERTON
COPGROVE
Ouseburn
DACRE
DARLEY
NIDD BRIDGE
KNARESBORO'
GOLDSBORO
ALLERTON
HAMMERTON
CATTAL
WILSTROP
HARROGATE
STARBECK
BENINGBROUGH
HAXBY
STRENSALL
FLAXTON
BARTON HILL
KIRKHAM ABBEY
HUTTONS AMBO
EARSWICK
WARTHILL
HOLTBY
Blubberhouses
ADDINGHAM
ILKLEY
BEN RHYDDING
BURLEY
OTLEY
PANNAL
SPOFFORTH
MARSTON MOOR
HESSAY
POPPLETON
YORK
FOSS ISLANDS GOODS
WETHERBY
WEETON
COLLINGHAM BRIDGE
THORP ARCH
NEWTON KYME
COPMANTHORPE
NABURN
TADCASTER
ARTHINGTON
BARDSEY
THORNER
STUTTON
BOLTON PERCY
ESCRICK
ULLESKELF
MENSTON
GUISELEY
YEADON
SHIPLEY
BRADFORD
LEEDS
HORSFORTH
HEADINGLEY
SCHOLES
ABERFORD
GARFORTH
MICKLEFIELD
SOUTH MILFORD
CHURCH FENTON
CAWOOD
RICCALL
WISTOW
SELBY
SHERBURN IN ELMET
CROSS GATES
MILFORD JUNC.
HAMBLETON
KIPPAX
LEDSTONE
BURTON SALMON
HEMINGBROUGH
WRESSLE
HOWDEN
BARMBY
DRAX
CARLTON
MORLEY
BATLEY
METHLEY
CASTLEFORD
KNOTTINGLEY
TEMPLE HIRST
DEWSBURY
NORMANTON
WAKEFIELD
PONTEFRACT
FEATHERSTONE
ACKWORTH
WOMERSLEY
HECK
BALNE
HUDDERSFIELD
KIRK SMEATON
NOSTELL
NORTON
ASKERN
MOSS
THORNE
KIRKBURTON
HEMSWORTH
HOLMFIRTH
CUDWORTH
STAINFORTH
BARNSLEY
STAIRFOOT
PENISTONE
DONCASTER
SPROTBORO
DENABY
CONISBORO
WATH
SWINTON
MEXBORO
FINNINGLEY
CHAPELTOWN
PARKGATE
ROTHERHAM ROAD
ROTHERHAM
TICKHILL
BAWTRY
ROSSINGTON
CENTRAL
WOODHEAD
DUNFORD BRIDGE
HAZLEHEAD BRIDGE
G.N. & G.E. JOINT
H.B. & W.R.
L. & Y.
MID

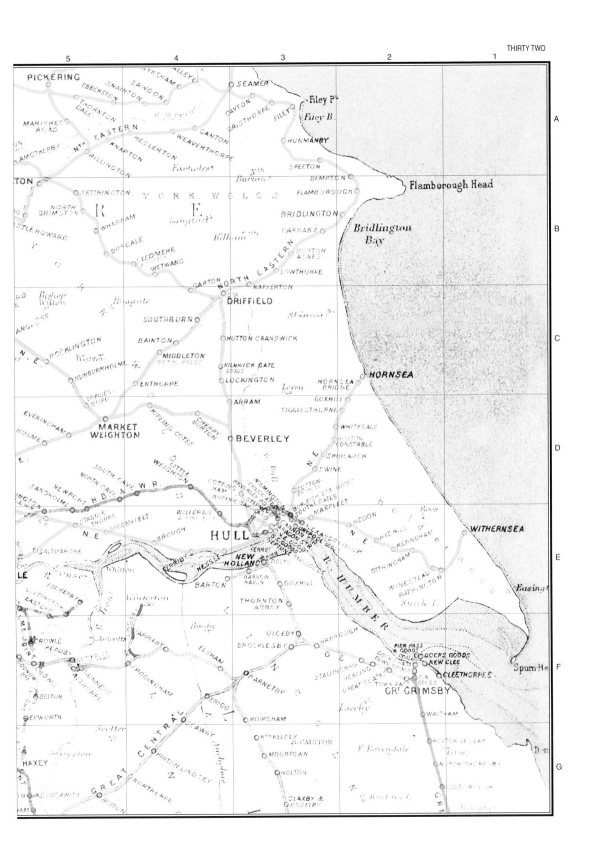

5   4   3   2   1

A

B

C

D

E

F

G

PICKERING
WYKEHAM
ALLEY
SEAMER
SNAINTON
SAWDON
EBBERSTON
CAYTON
THORNTON
DALE
GRISTHORPE
FILEY
Filey Pr
Filey B.
MARISHES
ROAD
WEAVERTHORPE
HUNMANBY
EASTERN
HESLERTON
GANTON
RAMOTHERBY
N.th
RILLINGTON
KNAPTON
SPEETON
TON
Foxholes
Nth
Burton
BEMPTON
SETTRINGTON
Y O R K   W O L D S
FLAMBOROUGH
Flamborough Head
NORTH
GRIMSTON
R   E
FLAMBOROUGH
WHARRAM
Langtoft
BRIDLINGTON
CASTLE HOWARD
Y
BUGDALE
CARNABY
Bridlington
Bay
LEDMERE
WETWANG
BURTON
AGNES
GARTON
NORTH EASTERN
LOWTHORPE
RD
Bishop
Wilton
Hugate
NAFFERTON
ANG
GOSS
DRIFFIELD
Skivan P.
SOUTHBURN
POCKLINGTON
Wods
BAINTON
HUTTON CRANSWICK
N. E.
NUNBURNHOLME
MIDDLETON
ON THE WOLDS
KILNWICK GATE
GOODS
LONDES
BORO
ENTHORPE
LOCKINGTON
Leven
HORNSEA
BRIDGE
HORNSEA
EVERINGHAM
ARRAM
GOXHILL
HOLME
MARKET
WEIGHTON
CHERRY
BURTON
KIPLING COTES
SIGGLESTHORPE
WHITEDALE
LITTLE
WEIGHTON
BEVERLEY
N. E.
BURTON
CONSTABLE
SOUTH CAVE
SKIRLAUGH
NORTH CAVE
H. B. & W. R.
SWINE
NEWPORT
WILMINGTON
SANDHOLME
STADDL
THORPE
COTTING
HAM
PAVLIEY ROAD
SUTTON
BRIDGE
INGTON
R. C.
BARCOMFLEET
BOTANIC STR
STEPNEY
BIRLEIGH STR GOODS
ROOS
HEDON
N. E.
SALTMARSHE
N. E.
WILLERBY
& KIRK ELLA
BROUGH
SOUTHCOATES
MARFLEET
PRESTON
N. E.
BURTON
WHITTON
FERRIBY
HESSLE
HULL
CANNON POOL
PARAGON STR
ST. GOODS
NEW
HOLLAND
STEPNEY
DRYPOOL
ALEXANDRA DOCK
MYTON DOCK
KEYINGHAM
OTTRINGHAM
WITHERNSEA
BARTON
BARROW
HAVEN
GOXHILL
DOCKS STR GOODS
FERRY
R. HUMBER
WINESTEAD
PATRINGTON
Easing
ROCKERBY
Whitton
THORNTON
ABBEY
Sunk I.
Winterton
R. Trent
Routby
ULCEBY
HARROUGH
CROWLE
KEADBY
Amcotts
APPLEBY
ELSHAM
BROCKLESBY
G. C.
PIER PASS
& GOODS
DOCKS GOODS
GOODNOW
BRT
NME
JOINT
CROWLE
FOCKERBY
EASTOFT
WOLLER STR RD
FROGINGHAM
HARROGHT
HEALING
BOCK & COAL
TOWN GOODS
DOCKS GOODS
NEW CLEE
WATER STR RD
BELTON
SCUNNESS
THORPE
CROWLE
BARNETBY
STALLINGBO
GREAT COATES
TOWN PASS
TOWN GOODS
G. N.
GOODS
CLEETHORPES
Spurn Hd
EPWORTH
FRIGG
HOWSHAM
GR GRIMSBY
HAXEY
Scotter
CENTRAL
SCAWBY
Nth KELSEY
Sth CAISTOR
Laceby
WALTHAM
HOLTON LE CLAY
Tetney
Silverston
KIRTON LINDSEY
MOORTOWN
F. Ravendale
NORTH THORESBY
NT
HAXEY
LOCKWITH
NORTHORPE
HOLTON
Birthorpe
HAM
BARTON
CLAXBY &
USSELBY
Miningbu

1   2   3   4   5

L. & N.W. & MID.

CROSSMICHAEL

LOCHANHEAD

KILLYWHAN

RUTHWELL

SOUTH WESTERN

ANNAN
CAL.

KIRKGUNZEON

CUMMERTREES

DUR
POR
CARLIS

CASTLE DOUGLAS
JUNC STA.

SOUTHWICK

SOLWAY VIADUCT
BOWNESS
CAL

STA

DALBEATTIE

G. & S.W.

BRIDGE of DEE

WHITRIGG

N.B.

STA

TARFF

KIRKIR

KIRKCUDBRIGHT

SILLOTH

ABBEY HOLME
JUNC. STA.

BLACK DYKE

ABBEY TOWN

CAL

CARLISLE

BROMFIELD

LEEGATE

KIRKBR

SOLWAY FIRTH

Allonby

BRAYTON
STA

JUNC.

HIGH B

CUMBR

Esk.

BULL GILL

MARYPORT

ASPATRIA

BAGGROW

MEALSG TE

DEARHAM BRIDGE

ELIZABETH DOCK
SENHOUSE DOCK

DEARHAM

MARYPORT

LINEFOOT
STA & JUNC

GOODS

COCKERMOUTH

EMBLETON

BASSENTHW E
LAKE

FLIMBY

GREAT BROUGHTON

PAPCASTLE

Skid

SIDDICK
EXCHANGE STA
DOCK

SEATON

L. & N.W.

BRIGHAM
JOINT STA

MARRON JN.

BRIGHAM
BRIDGEFOOT

R. Cocker

COCKERMOUTH

B

LONSDALE DOCK
MERCHANTS QUAY
STA

WORKINGTON

CAMER TURN
WR BRIDGE
CENTRAL

BULLGILL

BRANTHWAITE

MARRON

BRIDGEFOOT

Derwen
Water

DERWENT IRON W RS
MOSS BAY IRON W RS

HARRINGTON
BAIN'S TRAMWAY

HIGH HARR N
DISTINGTON

BULLOCK

Lows

Crummock W?

PARTON
STA

OATLANDS

LAMPLUGH

WHITEHAVEN
BRANSTY L.& N.W.
PRESTON STR. GOODS

C.&W.JCT

MORESBY
PARKS

ARLECDON

ROWRAH

KELTON FELL

Buttermere

CORKICKLE
MIRE HOUSE J N

LEATOR
MOOR

WINDER
YEATHOUSE

R.&K.F.

St Bees H d

C. & W. JCT.

GOODS

BRETT
FRIZINGTON

Ennerdale

Pillar

Gr Gab

MOOR ROW

GOODS
GOODS

SAINT BEES

W.C.&E.J.

WOODEND
GILLFOOT GOODS

EGREMONT

Scafell Pikes

NETHERTOWN

FURN. J.

BECKERMET

U

Wast Wr

Scafell

BRAYSTONES

SELLAFIELD

Gosforth

R

R. Ehen

ESKDALE

BOOT

SEASCALE

R.GLASS

BECKFOOT

ESKDALE GREEN

Old
CO

DRIGG

MUNCASTER

IRTON ROAD

FURN.

RAVENGLASS

R & E

Uphau

TOR

ESKMEALS

FURNESS

R. Duddon

BOOTLE

WD
LAN

BROUGHT

FOXFIELD

GREEN ROAD

SILECROFT

MILLOM

KIR B

UL

5   4   3   2   1

A
KIRKPATRICK
SCOTCH DYKE
Shank Castle
BARRASF
Houghton
JRSTONES
NCHOL
GRETNA GREEN
LONGTOWN
HAYDON BRIDGE
WALL
GRETNA
Kirklinton
R. Irthing
FLORISTON
LYNESIDE
GILSLAND
HALTWHISTLE
BARDON MILL
Langwost Priory
NAWORTH
LOW ROW
GREENHEAD
R. South Tyne
ELRINGTON
HEXH
ROCKCLIFFE
HARKER
BRAMPTON JUNC.
LANGLEY
DRUMBURGH
HOW MILL
FEATHERSTONE PARK
BURGH
HEADS NOOK
WETHERAL
COANWOOD
STAWARD
KIRKANDREWS
NORTH EASTERN
BISHOPHILL COL.
LAMBLEY
ALLENDALE

B
CARLISLE
CITADEL
SCOTBY
Cold Fell
Whitfield
R. Allen
Aikton
CUMMERS DALE
CUMWHINTON
SLAGGYFORD
Blanchland
DALSTON
COTEHILL
WREAY
Croglin
ALSTON
CURTHWAITE
Allenheads

C
WIGTON
ARMATHWAITE
Black Fell
Nenthead
WEARHEAD
D
SOUTHWAITE
Sebergham
Garrigill
ST JOHNS CHAPEL
WESTGATE WEARDALE
EASTGATE
CALTHWAITE
BURROSWALD
LAZONBY & KIRKOSWALD
Inglewood
CALDBECK
FLUMPTON
Forest
LITTLE SALKELD
Cross Fell
Skelton
LANGWATHBY

D
BLENCOW
PENRITH
CULGAITH
R. Tees
Caldron Snout
High Force
MIDDLETON IN TEESDALE
KESWICK
Saddleback
TROUTBECK
NEW BIGGIN
MICKLETO
THRELKELD
CLIFTON
NTH. EASTERN
LONG MARTON
Little Fell
KESWICK & PENRITH
PENRUDDOCK
CLIFTON & LOWTHER
CLIBURN
TEMPLE SOWERBY
APPLEBY
Ullswater
Lowther Castle
KIRKBY THORE
Ellswater

E
Thirlmere
Helvellyn
Patterdale
ORMSIDE
WARCOP
BROUGH
Wythburn
Brothers Water
High Street
Hawes Water
SHAP
Crosby Ravensworth
MUSGRAVE
BARRAS
Stainmore For
Grasmere
Rydal W.
CROSBY GARRETT
SMARDALE
Langdale Pikes
Shap Fells
GAISGILL
N E
KIRKBY STEPHEN

F
Man
HAWKSHEAD
AMBLESIDE
Low Wood
TEBAY
RAVENSTONE DALE & RAVENSTONEDALE
Wild Boar Fell
High Seat
NISTON LAKE
WINDERMERE
STAVELEY
MUKER
VER
L. & N.W.
Bowness
LOW GILL
BURNESIDE
GRAYRIGG
R. Eden
KENDAL
SEDBERGH
HAWES JUNC. & GARSDALE
HAWES
OXENHOLME
Rise Hill
ASHR

G
WINDERMERE LAKE SIDE
MIDDLETON
DENT
Widdale Fell
REENODD
HAVERTHWAITE
HEVERSHAM
Whernside
Blea Moor
SANDSIDE
MILNTHORPE
BARBON

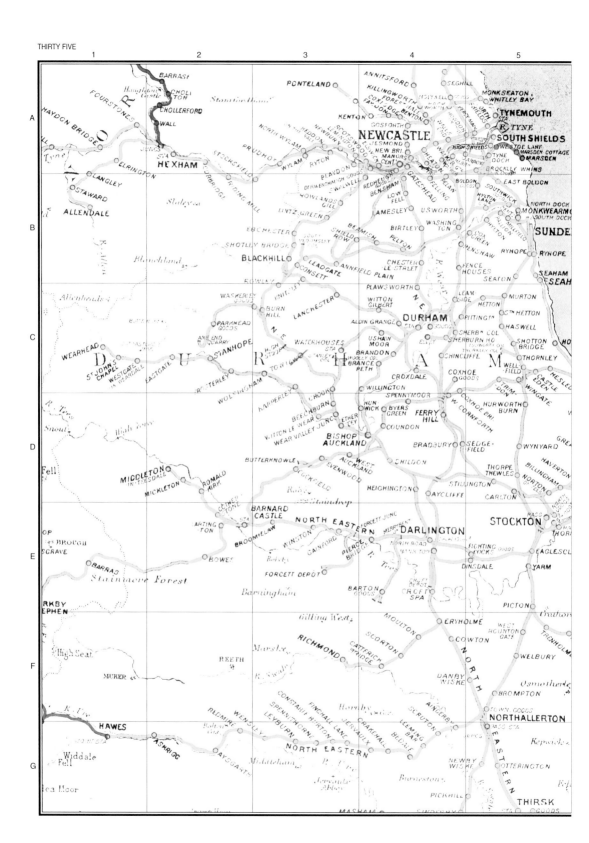

1   2   3   4   5

5 4 3 2 1

A

B

OUTH

RLAND

COL
AM

C

RDEN

HART

HARTLEPOOL
STA
VEST STA
Hartlepool
Bay
SEATON
CAREW.
Tees
Bay
ATHAM
D
PORT
CLARENCE
HILL
TOD
POINT
REDCAR
Tees Mouth
MARSKE
SALTBURY
GRANGETOWN
SOUTH BANK
BR TON
SKINNINGROVE
CARGO FLEET
MIDDLESBRO
NORTH
SKELTON
LOFTUS
EASINGTON
STAITHES
NEWPORT
ESTON
HINDERWELL
NABY
ORMESBY
GUISBRO
BOOSBE &
KETTLENESS
UPSALL
MINES
IFFE
Kunswick
Lythe
WHITBY
NUNTHORPE
PINCHING
THORPE
HUTTON GATE L
COMMO I
DALE
N
D
SANDSEND
WEST CLIFF
STA
CLE
GR AYTON
CA^LETON
E
NILDALE
DANBY
RUSWARP
SLEIGHTS
HAWSKER
STOKESLEY
INGLEBY
BATTERSBY
LS
LEALHOLM
N^M EASTERN
GLAISDALE
EGTON
GROSMONT
ROBIN HOOD'S
BAY
SEXHOW
FYLING
HALL
O TO
GOATHLAND
N E RAVENSCAR
BAR
CLEVELAND
EAST ROSEDALE
STAINTONDALE
HAYBURN WYKE
ROSEDALE
ABBEY
ROSEDALE
H
CLOUGHTON
A
M
B
L
E
T
O
N
NORTH   YOR K   M O O R S
Hawnby
Lastingham
SININGTON
CLEVISHAM
SCALBY
SCARBOROUGH
L & R. LIGHT
NORTH EASTERN
KIRBY
MOORSICE
E.
Richmond
FARM
HELMSLEY
NAW-ON
PICKERING
T BECKSTON
SNAINTON
SANDON
PERC. VALLEY
N YELLAM
SEAMER

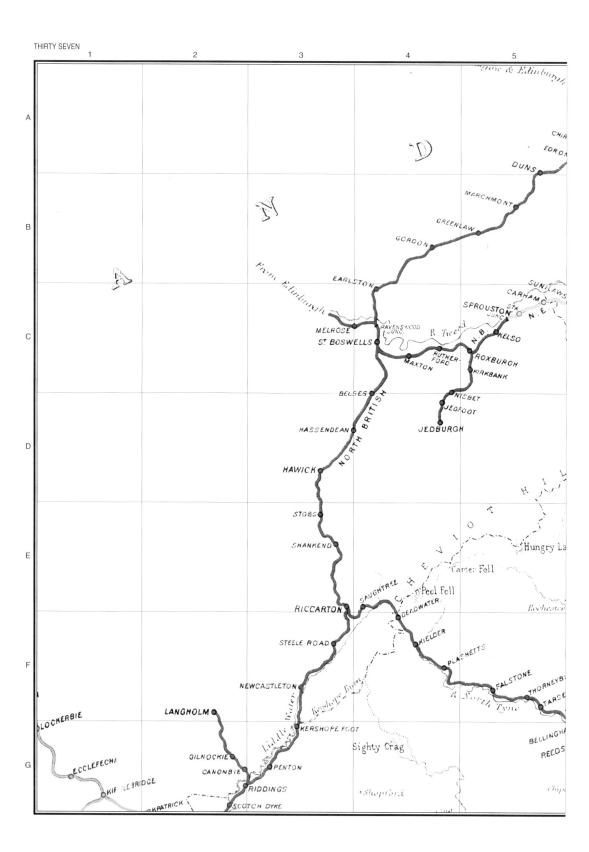

5   4   3   2   1

A

B

C

D

E

F

G

EYEMOUTH
STA.
BURNMOUTH
RESTON
AYTON
NORTH BRITISH
RNSIDE

BERWICK
DOCK
TWEEDMOUTH
STA.
R. Tweed
VELVET
HALL
SCREMERSTON
NORHAM
GOSWICK
TWIZELL
BEAL
Holy I.
Lowick
Old Law
COLDSTREAM
Ford
Staples I.
SMEAFIELD
Bugle
B.
Farne I.
Floddey
R. Till
MINDRUM
BELFORD
NORTH EASTERN
SEAHOUSES
Doddington
LUCKER
NORTH SUNDERLAND
KIRKNEWTON
AKELD
WOOLER
NEWHAM
CHATHILL
Beadnell B.
Chillingham
ILDERTON
CHRISTON BANK
Embleton B.
The Cheviot
Dunstanburgh
Castle
WOOPERTON
Eglingham
LITTLE MILL
EDGELEY
LONGHOUGHTON
GLANTON
R. Aln
ALNWICK
Windygate
Hill
WHITTINGHAM
Castle
STA.
ALNMOUTH
Bay
Shilbottle
ELLINGHAM
WARKWORTH
Warkworth Harb.
R. Coquet
Mwinton
AMBLE
aw
ROTHBURY
ACKLINGTON
BROOMHILL
BRINKBURN
R. Coquet
Felton
Druridge
AMBLE BRANCH
Bay
CHEVINGTON
R. Rede
Otterburn
Longhorsley
WIDDRINGTON
Cresswell
Snab Pt.
EWESLEY
LONGHIRST
ASHINGTON
NEWBIGGIN
BY-THE-SEA
WOODBURN
KNOWESGATE
LONG WITTON
Wansbeck
PEGSWOOD
NTH.
SEATON
Camboise
B.
SCOTSGAP
N. BRITISH
MORPETH
STA.
HEPSCOTT
MIDDLETON
ANGERTON
MELDON
CHOPPING
TON
BEDLINGTON
SLUTH
BLYTH
NORTH
STANNINGTON
BEBSIDE
NEWSHAM
SMOUTH
BRITISH
Belsay
R. Blyth
PLESSEY
HARTLEY
WARK
CRAMLINGTON
SEATON
DELAVAL
SEGHILL
BARRASFORD
ANNITSFORD
MONKSEATON
CHOLLER
PONTELAND
KILLINGWORTH
WHITLEY BAY
CO. FORC

1   2   3   4   5

A FLITWICK HENLOW THREE COUNTIES BALDOCK Barkway NEWPORT THAXTED
HARLINGTON HITCHIN Weston Graveley BUNTINGFORD ELSENHAM STANSTED
LEAGRAVE STEVENAGE WESTMILL BRAUGH STANDON BISHOPS STORTFORD DUNMO
DUNSTABLE LUTON KNEBWORTH HADHAM TAKELY EASTON LODGE
CHILTERN GREEN WELWYN WIDFORD SAWBRIDGEWORTH
B HARPENDEN LUTON HOO WHEATHAMPSTEAD HERTFORD WARE MARDOCK HARLOW High Easter
REDBOURN AYOT St MARGARET'S BURNT MILL Matching
HEMEL HEMPSTEAD HATFIELD HERTINGFORD BURY RYE HOUSE ROYDON CHEL
St ALBANS COLE GREEN HODDESDON BROXBOURNE Potter Street
C BOXMOOR PARK STREET POTTERS BAR THEOBALDS GROVE CHESHUNT NORTHWEALD BLAKE HALL ONGAR
KINGS LANGLEY BRICKET WOOD RADLETT ELSTREE FURTY HILL EPPING THEYDON BOIS INGATESTONE
METROPOLITAN WATFORD HADLEY WOOD ENFIELD LOCK CHIGWELL LANE SHENFIELD & HUTTON
RICKMANSWORTH BUSHEY HIGH BARNET NEW BARNET ENFIELD BRIMSDOWN LOUGHTON BRENTWOOD
D NORTHWOOD PINNER STANMORE WOODSIDE PARK TOTTERIDGE PONDERS END CHINGFORD BUCKHURST HAROLD WOOD
DENHAM HARROW RUISLIP EDGWARE FINCHLEY PALACE GATES WOODFORD CHIGWELL ROMFORD EAST HORNDON
UXBRIDGE GREENFORD SUDBURY HENDON HIGHGATE TOTTENHAM FAIRLOP UPMINSTER TILBURY
ICKENHAM WEMBLEY PARK SNARESBROOK LEYTON HORNCHURCH
WEST DRAYTON WILLESDEN JUNC KENTISH HACKNEY LEYTONSTONE ILFORD DAGENHAM
E LANGLEY HANWELL EALING PADDINGTON St PANCRAS STRATFORD BARKING OCKENDON
LONDON KINGS CROSS VICTORIA DKS BECKTON RAINHAM THAMES
BRENTFORD CHARING CROSS LONDON BRIDGE GALLIONS WOOLWICH BELVEDERE PURFLEET GRAYS
DATCHET ISLEWORTH HAMMERSMITH VICTORIA CANNON STR ERITH TILBURY
COLNBROOK HOUNSLOW BARNES WATERLOO PECKHAM GREENWICH ABBEY WOOD GREENHITHE
STAINES FELTHAM RICHMOND CLAPHAM JUNC HERNE HILL BLACKHEATH WELLING DARTFORD GRAV
EGHAM TWICKENHAM TOOTING DULWICH LEE NEW ELTHAM BEXLEY ROCHESTER SOUTHFLEET
VIRGINIA WATER HAMPTON KINGSTON BALHAM GROVE PARK ELTHAM SIDCUP CHISLEHURST MEOPHAM
F CHERTSEY WIMBLEDON NORWOOD BROMLEY SOUTH EASTERN
ADDLESTONE NORBITON MITCHAM SOUTH BECKENHAM MARY CRAY SWANLEY FARNINGHAM RD
CHERTSEY WEYBRIDGE SURBITON CARSHALTON CROYDON ORPINGTON CHELSFIELD LYNSFORD
WOKING BYFLEET COBHAM EWELL SUTTON PURLEY KNOCKHOLT SHOREHAM Stansted
HORSLEY CLAYGATE EPSOM BANSTEAD WARLINGHAM OTFORD DUNTON GREEN WROTHAM
EFFINGHAM JUNC ASHTEAD EPSOM DOWNS TATTENHAM CORNER BRASTED BAT & BALL
WORPLESDON LEATHERHEAD TADWORTH KINGSWOOD WOLDINGHAM SEVENOAKS WESTERHAM
BOOKHAM BOX HILL CATERHAM Knole Park
G GUILDFORD DORKING REIGATE MERSTHAM OXTED HILDENBORO TONBRIDGE
GOMSHALL BETCHWORTH REDHILL EARLSWOOD EDENBRIDGE
BRAMLEY HOLMWOOD NUTFIELD COLDSTONE HEVER PENSHURST SOUTHBORO PADD
Leith Hill HOPLEY LINGFIELD Ide Hill
GATWICK DORMANS COWDEN

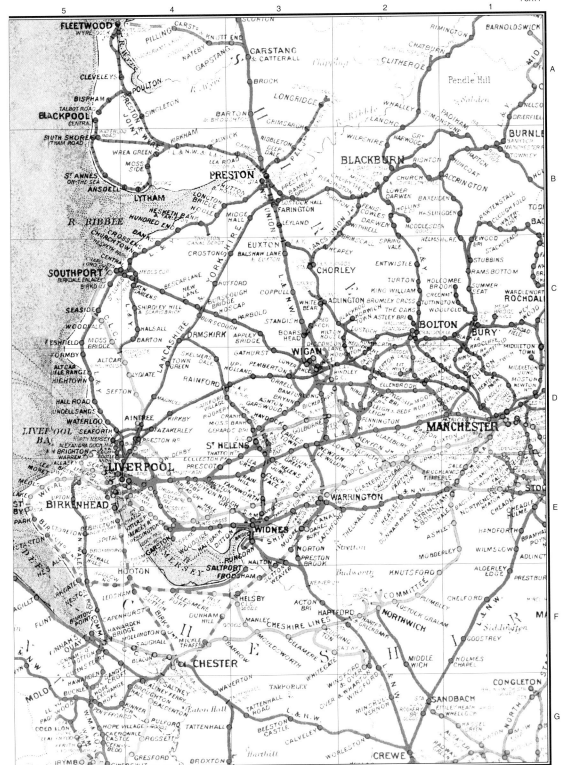

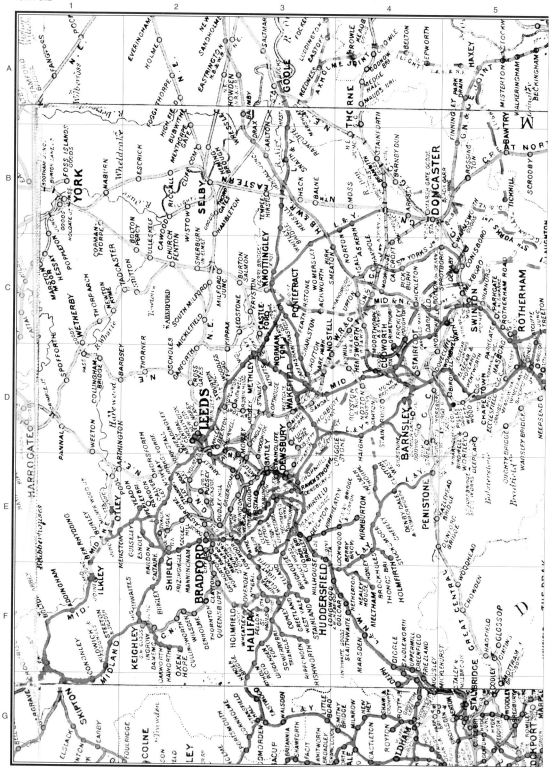

LIST OF ABBREVIATIONS

(In the case of Joint or Subsidiary Lines with individual titles, the owning or leasing partners or Companies are indicated in brackes irnmediately after the title.)

A&LR	Axminster & Lyme Regis	LB&SC	London, Brighton & South Coast
AD&R	Alexandra (Newport & South Wales) Docks & Railway	LD&EC	Lancashire, Derbyshire & East Coast
AN	Ashby & Nuneaton Joint (L&NW and Midland)	LT&S	London Tilbury & Southend
		M&SWJ	Midland & South Western Junction
B&A	Basingstoke & Alton Light	Met	Metropolitan
B&M	Brecon & Merthyr	Mid&GN	Midland & Great Northern Joint (GN and Midland)
BW&A	Bideford, Westward Ho! & Appledore	Mid	Midland
		MSJ&A	Manchester South Junction & Altrincham (GC and L&NW)
C&W	Carnforth & Wennington Joint (Furness and Midland)		
C&WJ	Cleator & Workington Junction	N&SJ	Norfolk & Suffolk Joint (GE and Mid&GN)
Cam	Cambrian	NB	North British
CLC	Cheshire Lines Committee (GC, GN and Midland)	NE	North Eastern
CV	Colne Valley	NL	North London
		NS	North Staffordshire
E&WJn	East & West Junction	NW	North Wales Narrow Gauge
Furn	Furness	P&W	Preston & Wyre
FYN	Freshwater, Yarmouth & Newport	PB&M	Padstow, Bedruthan & Mawgan
G&SW	Glasgow & South Western	R&SB	Rhondda & Swansea Bay
GC	Great Central		
GE	Great Eastern	S&D	Somerset & Dorset Joint Committee (L&SW and Midland)
GN	Great Northern		
GV	Glyn Valley	S&H	Shrewsbury & Hereford Joint (GW and L&NW)
GW	Great Western		
		S&M	Swansea & Mumbles
HB&WR	Halifax, Barnsley & West Riding	SE&C	South Eastern & Chatham
		StA&P	St Austell & Pentewan
IoWCen	Isle of Wight Central Railway		
		TV	Taff Vale
KT&T	Kelvedon, Tiptree & Tollesbury Pier		
		W&C	Weston, Clevedon & Portishead
L&NW	London & North Western	W&M	Wrexham & Minera Joint (GW and L&NW)
L&SW	London & South Western		
L&R	Lastingham & Rosedale	WC&EJ	Whitehaven, Cleator & Egremont Joint (Furness and L&NW)
L&Y	Lancashire & Yorkshire		

INDEX

Station	Grid Ref
Balne	27A3/31E4
Balshaw Lane & Euxton	30E4/40B3
Bamber Bridge	30E4/40B3
Bamford	26B3
Bamfurlong	25A3/30G4/40D3
Bampton (Devon)	2A1/3C2/9G5
Bampton (Oxon)	11D5
Banbury (GW)	12B5
Banbury (L&NW)	12B5
Bangor	23B3
Bangor-on-Dee	24D2/25E2
Bankfield	24A2/25A1/40D5
Banks	30E5
Banstead & Burgh Heath	6A1/7C1/39F3
Barber's Bridge	11C1/18F2
Barbon	30A4/34G3
Barcombe	7F2
Barcombe Mills	7F2
Bardney	28E5
Bardon Mill	34A2/35A1
Bardon Hill	19C4/26G2
Bardsey	31D3
Bare Lane	30B5
Bargoed	10B5/16F1
Barham	8C3
Barking	7A2/13F3/39D4
Barkstone	20A3/27G5
Barlaston	25E5
Barmby	31E5
Barming	7C4
Barmouth	23F4
Barmouth Junction	23F4
Barnack	20C2
Barnard Castle	35E2
Barnby Dun	27B3/31F4
Barnehurst	7A3/13G4/39E4
Barnes	7A1/13G2/39E2
Barnetby	28B5/32F4
Barnham	21F5
Barnoldswick	30C2/40A1
Barnsley (L&Y)	27B1/31F2
Barnsley (Mid)	27B1/31F2
Barnstaple (GW)	9G2
Barnstaple Junction	9G2
Barnstaple Town	9G2
Barnstone	20A4
Barnt Green	19F1
Barnwell (Cambs)	13A3/21G2
Barnwell (Northants)	20E2
Barras	34E1/35E1
Barrasford	35A2/38G5
Barrow (CLC)	24B1/25C2/40F4
Barrow Central	29B4
Barrow Haven	28A5/32E4
Barrow Hill	26C2
Barrow-on-Soar & Quorn	19C5
Barry	10D5
Barry Dock	10D5
Barry Island	10D5
Bartlow	13B4
Barton (GC)	28A5/32E4
Barton Goods	35E4
Barton (L&Y)	29F5/40C4
Barton & Walton	19C3/26G3
Barton & Broughton	30D4/40A3
Barton Hill (Yorks)	31B5
Barton Moss	25A4/30G3/40D2
Barton-le-Street	31A5
Baschurch	24F1/25F2
Basford	19A5/26E1/27G3
Basingstoke	5A5
Bason Bridge	3A5/10F3
Bassaleg (B&M)	10C4
Bassaleg (GW)	10C4
Bassenthwaite Lake	33D5
Bat & Ball	7C3/39F5
Bath (GW)	11G1
Bath (Mid)	11G1
Bathampton	11G1
Batley	31E2
Batley Carr	31E2
Batley East	31E1
Battersby	36F5
Battle	7F5
Bawtry	27C3
Baxenden	30E3/40B1
Bay Horse	30C5
Baynards	6C3
Beaconsfield	12E2
Beal	38B4
Bealings	14A2
Beamish	35B4
Bearley	19G3
Bearsted	7C5
Beauchieff	26B2/27D1
Beaufort	10A4/16E1
Beaulieu Road	5E3
Bebington & New Ferry	24A2/25B1/40E5
Bebside	38G2
Beccles	22E2
Beck Holes	36F3
Beckenham	7B2/13G3/39E3
Beckermet	33E4
Beckfoot	33F5
Beckford	11B2
Beckingham	27D4
Beckton	7A2/13F3/39D4
Bedale	35G4
Bedford (L&NW)	12A1
Bedford (Mid)	12A1
Bedlington	38F2
Bedlinog	10B5/16F2
Bedminster	10D1
Bedwas	10B4/16G1
Bedwellty Pits	16F2
Bedwelty Pits	10A4/16F1
Bedworth	19E4
Bedwyn	11G4
Beechburn	35D3
Beeston (Notts)	19A5/26E1
Beeston (Yorks)	31E2
Beeston Castle	24C1/25D3/40G3
Beighton	26B2/27D2
Bekesbourne	8C3
Belford	38C3
Belgrave & Birstall	19C5
Bellbusk	30C2
Belle Vue	25A5/30G2/40D1
Bellingham (North Tyne)	38F5
Belmont	6A1/7B1/39F3
Belper	26E2/27G1
Belses	37D4
Belton (Lincs)	27B4
Belton (Norfolk)	22D2
Belvedere	7A3/13F3/39E4
Bembridge	5F5
Bempton	32A3
Ben Rhydding	31C1
Benfleet	7A5
Bengeworth	11A3
Beningbrough	31B4
Bensham	35B4
Bentham	30B3
Bentley (Hants)	6B5
Bentley (Suffolk)	14B3
Benton	35A4
Benwick	21E1
Bere Alston	2E5
Bere Ferrers	2E5
Berkeley	10B1
Berkeley Road	10B1
Berkhamsted	12D1/39B1
Berkswell	19E3
Berney Arms	22D2
Berrington	24G1
Berrington & Eye	18C4
Berry Brow	31F1
Berwick (Northumb)	38A4
Berwick (Sussex)	7F3
Berwyn	24D3
Bescar Lane	30F5/40C4
Bescot	19D1
Bestwood Colliery	26E1/27G2
Betchworth	6A2/7C1/39G2
Bethesda	23C4
Betley Road	24C1
Bettisfield	24E1/25E2
Bettws (Llangeinor)	9C5/16G3
Bettws Garmon	23C3
Betws-y-Coed	23C5
Beverley	32D4
Beverley Rd	28A5/32D3
Bewdley	18C2
Bexhill (LB&SC)	7F4
Bexhill (SE&C)	7F4
Bexley	7B3/13G4/39E4
Bexleyheath	7A3/13G3/39E4
Bicester	12C4
Bickershaw	25A3/30G4/40D3
Bickleigh	2E4
Bickley	7B2/13G3/39E4
Biddenden	7D5
Biddulph	25D5/40G1
Bideford (BW&A)	9G1
Bideford	9G2
Bidford	11A3/19G2
Bidston	24A3/25A1/40E5
Biggleswade	13B1
Bigs Weir	10A2
Billacombe	2F4
Billericay	13E5
Billing	20G4
Billingborough	20A2
Billingham	35D5
Billingshurst	6C3
Bilson Goods	18G3
Bilston	18A1/19D1
Binegar	4A5/10E1
Bingham Road	20A5/27G4
Bingham	20A5/27G4
Bingley	31D1
Binton	11A3/19G2
Birchills	19D1
Birchington-on-Sea	8B3/14G2
Birdbrook	13B5
Birdingbury	19E4
Birdwell	26A2/27C1/31G2
Birdwell & Wortley	26A3/27C1/31G2
Birkdale	29F5/40C5
Birkdale Palace	29F5/40C5
Birkdale	29F5/40C5
Birkenhead Central	24A2/25B1/40E5
Birkenhead Docks	24A2/25B1/40E5
Birkenhead Hamilton Square	24A2/25B1/40E5
Birkenhead Park	24A2/25B1/40E5
Birkenhead Town	24A2/25B1/40E5
Birkenhead Woodside	24A2/25B1/40E5
Birkenshaw	31E1
Birley	26B2
Birmingham New Street	19E2
Birmingham Snow Hill	19E2
Birstall	31E1
Birstwith	31B2
Birtley	35B4
Bishop Auckland	35D4
Bishop's Lydeard	3B3/10G4
Bishop's Nympton & Molland	3B1/9G4
Bishop's Waltham	5D5
Bishop's Castle	18B5
Bishops Bourne	8C3
Bishops Stortford	13C3/39B4
Bishopstone	7G2
Bispham	29D5/40A5
Bitterley	18C3
Bitterne	5D4
Bitton	10D1
Blaby	19D5
Black Bank	21E2
Black Bull	25D5/40G1
Black Dyke	31D5
Black Mill	9C5/16G3
Blackburn	30E3/40B2/24E2
Blackburn (L&NW Goods)	30E3/40B2
Blackheath	7A2/13G3/39E4
Blackhill	35B3
Blackmoor	9F3
Blackpool Central	29D5/40A5
Blackrod	30F4/40C2
Blackwall	7A2/13F3/39D4
Blackwater & York Town	6A4
Blackwater (IoW)	5F4
Blackwell	19F1
Blackwood	10B4/16F1
Blacon	24C2/25C2/40F4
Blaenau Ffestiniog (FR)	23D4
Blaenau Ffestiniog (GW)	23D4
Blaenau Ffestiniog (L&NW)	23D4
Blaenavon (GW)	10A4
Blaenavon (L&NW)	10A4
Blaengarw	9B5/16G3
Blaengwynfy	9B5/16F3
Blaenrhondda	9B5/16F3
Blagdon	10E2
Blaina	10A4/16F1
Blake Hall	13E4/39C5
Blake Street	19D2
Blakeney	10A1
Blakesley	12A4
Blandford	4D3
Blankney & Metheringham	28F5
Blaydon	35A3
Bleadon & Uphill	10E3
Bleasby	27F4
Bledlow	12D3
Blencow	34D4
Blenheim & Woodstock	12C5
Bletchington	12C5
Bletchley	12B2
Blidworth & Rainworth	27F3
Blisworth	12A3/20G5
Blockley	11B4
Blodwell Junction	24F3
Blowick	29F5/40C4
Bloxham	12B5
Bloxwich	19D1
Blue Anchor	3A2
Bluestone	22B4
Blundellsands	25A1/29G5/40D5
Blunham	13A1
Blunsdon	11E3
Bluntisham	21F1
Blyth	38G2
Blythburgh	22F2
Blythe Bridge	19A1/26E5

Place	Ref
Blyton	27C5/32G5
Boar's Head	30F4/40C3
Bodfari	24B4
Bodiam	7E5
Bodmin (GW)	1E4
Bodmin (L&SW)	1E4
Bodorgan	23B2
Bognor	6E4
Boldon Goods	35B5
Bollington	26B5
Bolsover (LD&EC)	26C1/27E2
Bolsover (Mid)	26C1/27E2
Bolton (L&NW)	30B5/40C2
Bolton Percy	31D4
Bolton Craddock Lane	30F3/40C2
Bolton-le-Sands	30B5
Bolton-on-Dearne	26A1/27C2/31G3
Boncath	15C3
Bond's Main	26C2/27E2
Bont Newydd	23F5
Bookham	6A2/39F2
Boosbeck	36E4
Boot	33F5
Bootle (Cumb)	33G4
Bootle (L&NW)	24A3/25A1/29G5/40D5
Bootle (L&Y)	24A3/25A1/29G5/40D5
Bordesley	19E2
Bordon	6B5
Boroughbridge	31B3
Borrowash	19A4/26F2
Borth	17B1
Borwick	30A4
Boscombe	4E1/5F2
Bosham	6E5
Bosley	26C5
Boston	21A1/28G3
Botanic Gardens (Hull)	28A5/32E3
Botley	5D5/20A4/27G4
Bottisham & Lode	21G2
Boughrood	16C1/17E5
Boughton	27D3
Bourne End	12E2
Bourne	20B2
Bournemouth Central	4E1/5F1
Bournemouth West	4E1/5F1
Bournville	19E2
Bourton-on-the-Water	11C4
Bovey	2D2
Bow	2B3
Bow Street	17B1
Bowes	35E2
Bowes Park	13E2/39D3
Bowness	33A5
Box Hill	6B2/39G2
Box	11G1
Boxford	11F5
Boxhill & Burford Bridge	6A2/7C1/39G2
Boxmoor	2D1/39C1
Boyces Bridge	21D2
Braceboro Spa	20C2
Brackley (GC)	12B3
Brackley (L&NW)	12B4
Bracknell	12G2
Bradbury	35D4
Bradfield	14C3
Bradford (Mid)	31D1
Bradford City Road	31D1
Bradford Exchange	31D1
Brading	5F5
Bradley	31E1
Bradley & Moxley	18A1
Bradley Fold	30F3/40C1
Bradnop	26D5
Bradwell	12B2
Brafferton	31B3
Braintree	13C5
Braithwaite	33D5
Bramber	6D2/7F1
Bramford	14A3
Bramhall	25B5/40E1
Bramley (GW)	5A5
Bramley (GN)	31D2
Bramley & Wonersh	6B3/39G1
Brampford Speke	2B1/3D1
Brampton (Suffolk)	22E2
Brampton Goods (Derbys)	26C2/27E1
Brampton Junction	34A3
Bramwith	27B3/31F4
Brancepeth	35C4
Brandon (Co Durham)	21E4
Brandon (Norfolk)	21E4
Brandon & Wolston	19F4
Branksome	4E1/5F1
Bransford Road	11A1/18D2
Branston & Heighington	28E5
Branston	19B3/26G3
Branthwaite	33D4
Brasted	7C3/39F4
Bratton Fleming	9F3
Braughing	13C3/39A4
Braunston	19F5
Braunston & Willoughby	19F5
Braunton	9F2
Braystones	33E4
Brayton	33C5
Breadsall	19A4/26E2/27G1
Breamore	4C1/5D2
Brecon	16D2/17F4
Bredbury	26A5
Bredon	11B2/18E1
Brent (Devon)	2E3
Brent Knoll	3A4/10E3
Brentford (GW)	13F1/39E2
Brentford (L&SW)	13F1/39E2
Brentor	2D4
Brentwood & Warley	13E4/39D5
Bretby	19B3
Brettell Lane	18B1/19E1
Bricket Wood	13E1/39C2
Bridestowe	2C4
Bridge	8C3
Bridge of Dee	33A2
Bridgefoot	33D4
Bridgend	9C5
Bridgnorth	18A2
Bridgwater (GW)	3B4/10G4
Bridgwater (S&D)	3B4/10F4
Bridlington	32B3
Bridport	3E5
Bridport East Street	3E5
Bridport West Bay	3E5
Brierfield	30D2/40A1
Brierley Hill	18B1/19E1
Brigg	28B5/32F4
Brigham	33D4
Brighouse	31E1
Brightlingsea	14D4
Brighton Road	19E2
Brighton Central	6E1/7G1
Brighton Kemp Town	6E1/7G1
Brighton Lewes Road	6E1/7F1
Brighton London Road	6E1/7G1
Brill	12C4
Brimscombe	11D2
Brimsdown	13E3/39C3
Brinkburn	38E4
Brinklow	19E4
Brinkworth	11F2
Brinscall	30E4/40B2
Brislington	10D1
Bristol Harbour Goods	10D2
Bristol St Philips	10D1
Bristol Temple Meads	10D1
Britannia	30E2/40A1
Brithdir	10B5/16F1
Briton Ferry Road	9B3/16F4
Briton Ferry (GW)	9B4/16F4
Briton Ferry (R&SB)	9B4/16F4
Brixham	2E2/3G1
Brixton	7A1/13G2/39E3
Brixton Road	2F4
Brixworth	20F4
Broad Clyst	2C1/3E2
Broad Green	24A2/25B2/40E4
Broadfield	30F2/40C1
Broadheath	25B4/40E1
Broadley	30F2/40A1
Broadstairs	8B2/14G1
Broadstone	4D2/5E1
Broadway	11B3
Broadwey	4E4
Brock	30D4/40A3
Brockenhurst	5E3
Brockholes	31F1
Brocklesby	28B5/32F3
Brockley Whins	35A5
Bromborough	24B2/25B1/40E4
Bromfield (Cumb)	33C5
Bromfield (Shrops)	18C4
Bromford Bridge	19E2
Bromley Cross	30F3/40C2
Bromley North	7B2/13G3/39E4
Bromley South	7B2/13G3/39E4
Bromsgrove	19F1
Bromshall	19A2/26F4
Bromyard	18D3
Bronwydd Arms	15D3
Brookland	8E5
Brooklands	25A5/40E1
Brooksby	20C5
Brookwood for Bisley Camp	6A4
Broom	11A3/19G2
Broome	18B5
Broomfleet	27A5/32E5
Broomhill	38E2
Broomielaw	35E3
Brotton	36E4
Brough	27A5/32E4
Broughton Cross	33D4
Broughton	29A4/33G5
Broughton Astley	19D5
Broughton Hall	24C2/25C1/40G4
Broughton Lane	26B2/27D1
Broughty Ferry	34E4
Browndown	5E5
Brownhills (L&NW)	19C2
Brownhills (Mid)	19C2
Broxbourne & Doddesdon	13D3/39C3
Broxton	24D1/25D2/40G4
Brundall	22D3
Brunswick	24A2/25B1/40E4
Bruton	4B4/10F1
Brymbo (GW)	24D3/40G5
Brymbo (WM&CO)	24D3/40G5
Bryn	9B4/16G4
Brynamman (GW)	9A3/16E4/17G2
Brynamman (Mid)	9A3/16E4/17G2
Brynglas	17A1/23G4
Bryngwyn (Camb)	24F3
Bryngwyn (NWNG)	23D3
Brynkir	23D3
Brynmawr	24F3
Brynmenyn	9C5/16G3
Brynn	25A3/30G4/40D3
Bubwith	31D5
Buckden	20F1
Buckenham	22D3
Buckfastleigh	2E3
Buckhurst Hill	13E3/39D4
Buckingham	12B3
Buckley	24C2/25C1
Bucknall	25E5
Bucknell	18C5
Bude	1B5
Budleigh Salterton	3E3
Bugle	1E3
Bugsworth	26B5
Buildwas	18A3
Builth Road (Cam)	16B2/17D4
Builth Road (L&NW)	16B2/17D4
Builth Wells	16B2/17E4
Bulford	4A1/5B2
Bulkington	19E4
Bull Gill	33C4
Bullo Pill	10A1/18G3
Bulwell	19A5/26E1/27G2
Bulwell Common	19A5/26E1/27G2
Bulwell Forest	19A5/26E1/27G2
Bungay	22E3
Buntingford	13C3/39A3
Burbage	5A2/11G4
Burdale	32B5
Bures	14B5
Burgess Hill	6D1/7F1
Burgh	28E2/34A5
Burghclere	5A4
Burleigh Street Goods	28A5
Burlescombe	3C3
Burley	31C1
Burn Hill	35C3
Burneside	34F4
Burngullow	1F3
Burnham	3A4/10E4
Burnham Beeches	12F2
Burnham Market	21A5
Burnham on Crouch	14E4
Burnley Bank Top	30D2/40B1
Burnley Barracks	30D2/40B1
Burnley Manchester Road	30D2/40B1
Burnmouth	38A5
Burnt Fen	21E3
Burnt House	21E1
Burnt Mill	13D3/39B4
Burrington	10E2
Burscough	30F5/40C4
Burscough Bridge	30F5/40C4
Bursledon	5D4
Burslem	25D5
Burston	22E4
Burton Constable	32D3
Burton & Holme	30A4/34G4
Burton Agnes	32B3
Burton Joyce	20A5/27C3
Burton Point	24B2/25C1/40F5
Burton Salmon	27A2/31E3
Burton-on-Trent	19B3/26F3
Burton-on-Trent Moor Street	19B3/26F3
Burwell	21G3
Bury High Level	30F2/40C1
Bury Low Level	30F2/40C1
Bury St Edmunds	21G5
Bush Hill Park	13E2/39C3
Bushbury	18A1/19D2
Bushey	13E1/39C2
Butler's Hill	26E1/27G2
Butterknowle	35D3
Butterley	26D2/27F1

Name	Ref	Name	Ref	Name	Ref	Name	Ref
Buttington	24G3/25G1	Carmarthen	15E5	Chatham Central	7B5	Christon Bank	38D3
Buxted	7E3	Carmarthen Town	15E5	Chathill	38C3	Christow	2C2/3E1
Buxton	26C4	Carn Brea	1A3/1G1	Chatteris	21E1	Christ's Hospital	
Buxton Lammas	22C4	Carnaby	30B5	Chatterley	25D5	(West Horsham)	6C2
Byers Green	35D4	Carnarvon	23C2	Cheadle (Ches)	25B5/40E1	Chudleigh	2D2/3F1
Byfield	12A5/19G5	Carnforth	30B5	Cheadle (Staffs)	19A1	Church & Oswaldtwistle	30E3/40B2
Byfleet & Woodham	6A3/39F1	Carno	17A4	Cheadle Hulme	25B5/40E1	Church Fenton	31D4
Bynea	9B2/16F5	Carr Mill	25A3	Cheam	6A1/7B1/39F3	Church Road (B&M)	10C4/16G1
		Carrington	26E1/27G3	Checker House	27D3	Church Road (CLC)	
Cadeleigh & Bickleigh	2B2/3D2	Carrog	24D4	Cheddar	10E2		24A2/25B2/40E4
Cadishead	25A4/30G3/40E2	Carshalton	7B1/13G2/39F3	Cheddington	12C2	Church Road (Mid)	19E2
Cadoxton	10D5	Castle Mill	24E3/25E1	Cheddleton	26D5	Church Stretton	18A4
Caerau	9B4/16F3	Castle Douglas	33A2	Chedworth	11D3	Church Village	10C5/16G2
Caergwrle Castle		Castle Ashby &		Chelfham	9F3	Churchbury	13E2/39C3
	24C2/25D1/40G5	Earl's Barton	20G4	Chelford	15A3/20D1/45B5	Churchdown	11C2/18G1
Caerleon	10B3	Castle Bromwich	19D2	Chellaston &		Churchill	18B1
Caerphilly	10C5/16G1	Castle Caereinion	17A5/24G3	Swarkestone	19B4/26F2	Churchtown	29E5/40C4
Caersws	17B4	Castle Cary	4B5/10G1	Chelmsford	13D5	Churchway	18G3
Caerwys	24B4	Castle Donington &		Chelsfield	7B3/13G3/39F4	Churn	12F5
Caister-on-Sea	22C1	Shardlow	19B5/26F1	Cheltenham (GW)	11C2/18F1	Churston	2E2
Calbourne & Shalfleet	5F4	Castle Eden	35C5	Cheltenham Lansdown	11C2/18F1	Churwell	31E2
Caldon Low	26D4	Castle Howard	31B5	Cheltenham		Chwilog	23E2
Callerton	35A3	Castleford (L&Y)	27A1/31E3	High Street	11C2/18F1	Cilfrew	9B4/16F4
Callington	2D5	Castleford (NE)	27A2/31E3	Chepstow	10B2	Cilfynydd	10B5/16G2
Calne	11G2	Castlethorpe	12A3	Chequeherbert	30F3/40D2	Cilmery	16B2/17E4
Calstock	2D5	Castleton (Cleveland)	36E4	Cherry Burton	32D4	Cinderford (GW)	10A1/18G3
Calthwaite	34C4	Castleton (L&Y)	30F2/40C1	Cherry Tree	30E3/40B2	Cinderford (S&W)	10A1/18G3
Calveley	25D3/40G3	Castletown	29G2	Chertsey	12G1/39F1	Cirencester (GW)	11D3
Calverley	31D1	Castor	20D2	Chesham	12D1	Cirencester (M&SWJ)	11D3
Calvert	12C3	Catcliffe	26B2/27D2	Cheshunt	13E3/39C3	Clacton-on-Sea	14D3
Cam	11E1	Caterham	6A1/39F3	Chester General	24C2/25C2/40F4	Clandon & Ripley	6A3/39F1
Camber	8E5	Catfield	22C2	Chester Liverpool Road		Clapham	30B3
Camberley &		Caton	30B4		24C2/25C2/40F4	Clapham Junction	7A1/13G2/39E3
York Town	6A4/12G2	Cattal	31C3	Chester Northgate		Clarbeston Road	14D2
Camborne	1A2/1G1	Causeland	1E5		24C2/25C2/40F4	Clatford	5B3
Cambridge (GE)	13A3/21G2	Cavendish	14A5	Chester Road	19D2	Claverdon	19F3
Cambridge (GN Goods)		Cawood	31D4	Chesterfield (GC)	26C2/27E1	Claxby & Usselby	28C5/32G3
	13A3/21G2	Cawston	22B4	Chesterfield (LD&EC)	26C2/27E1	Clay Cross	26C2/27E1
Cambridge (L&NW)	13A3/21G2	Caythorpe	27F5	Chesterfield Midland	26C2/27E1	Clay Cross	
Cambridge (Mid Goods)		Cayton	32A3	Chester-le-Street	35B4	Town Goods	26C2/27E1
	13A3/21G2	Cefn (B&M)	16E2	Chesterton	25D5	Claydon (Bucks)	12C3
Camelford	1C4	Cefn (GW)	24D3/25E1	Chettisham	21E2	Claydon (Suffolk)	14A3
Camerton	33D4	Cefn-y-Bedd	24C2/25D1/40G5	Chevington	38E3	Claygate	6A2/39F2
Camerton	10E1	Cemmes	17A3/23G5	Chichester (Selsey)	6E4	Claypole	27F5
Camphill	19F2	Cemmes Road	17A3/23G5	Chichester	6E4	Clayton	31D2
Cannock	26G5	Cerist	17B4	Chigwell Lane	13E3	Clayton West	31F2
Canonbie	37G2	Cerney & Ashton Keynes	11E3	Chigwell	13E3/39C4	Cleator Moor	33E4
Canterbury East	8C4	Chacewater	1F1	Chilcompton	10E1	Cleckheaton (L&Y)	31E1
Canterbury West	8C4	Chadwell Heath	7A3/13F3/39D4	Childwall	24A2/25B2/40E4	Cleckheaton (L&NW)	31E1
Cantley	22D2	Chagford	2C3/3F2	Chilham	8C4	Clee Hill	18C3
Capel	14B3	Chalcombe Road	12E1	Chiltern Green	13C1/39B2	Cleethorpes	28B3/32F2
Capel Bangor	17C1	Chalder	6E4	Chilvers Coton	19E4	Cleeve	11B2/18F1
Capenhurst	24B2/25C2/40F4	Chalfont Road	39C1	Chilworth & Albury	6B3/39G1	Clenchwarton	21C3
Carbean	1F3	Chalford	11D2	Chingford	13E3/39C4	Cleobury Mortimer	15C2
Carbis Bay	1A2	Challow	11E5	Chinnor	12D3	Clevedon (GW)	10D3
Carbus	1E3	Chandler's Ford	5D4	Chippenham	11F2	Clevedon (WC&P)	10D3
Carcroft	27B2/31F4	Chapel-en-le-Frith (L&NW)		Chipping Norton Junction	11C4	Cleveleys	29D5/40A4
Cardiff (Cardiff Rly)	10D4		26B4/31G2	Chipping Norton	11C5	Cliburn	34D3
Cardiff (GW)	10D4	Chapel-en-le-Frith (Mid)	26B4/31G2	Chipping Sodbury	1F1	Cliddesden	5B5
Cardiff Clarence Road	10D4	Chapelton	9G2	Chipstead	6A1/7C1/39F3	Cliff Common	31D5
Cardiff Docks	10D4	Chapeltown (GC)	26A2/27C1	Chirk (GVT)	24E3/25E1	Cliffe	7A4/13C5
Cardiff Queen Street	10C4	Chapeltown (Mid)	26A2/27C1	Chirk (GW)	24E3/25E1	Clifton Maybank Goods	4C5
Cardiff Riverside	10C4	Chappel	14C5	Chirnside	38A5	Clifton Mill	19F5
Cardigan	15C3	Chard Joint	3D4	Chiseldon	11F4	Clifton & Lowther	34D4
Cardington	12A1/13A1	Chard Junction	3D4	Chislehurst	7B2/13G3/39E4	Clifton (L&Y)	25A5/30F2/40D1
Cargo Fleet	36E5	Chard (L&SW)	3D4	Chollerford	35A2	Clifton (NE)	34D3
Carham	37C5	Charing	8C5	Chollerton	35A2/38G5	Clifton (NS)	19A2/26E4
Carisbrooke	5F4	Charlbury	11C5	Cholsey & Moulsford	12E4	Clifton Bridge	10D2
Cark in Cartmel	30A5	Charlton (Som)	7A2/13F3/39E4	Choppington	38F2	Clifton Down	10D2
Carlinghow	31E1	Charlton (London)	4B5/10G2	Chorley Junction	30E4/40C3	Clifton Rd	31E1
Carlisle Citadel	34B4	Charlton Kings	11C2/18G1	Chorley (L&NW Goods)		Clifton-on-Trent	27E4
Carlton (Co Durham)	35D5	Chartham	8C4		30E4/40C3	Clipston & Oxendon	20E4
Carlton (Yorks)	27A3/31E5	Chartley	19B1/26F5	Chorley Wood	12E1/39C1	Clipstone	27E3/41C5
Carlton & Netherfield	20A5/27G3	Charwelton	19G5	Chorlton-cum-Hardy		Clitheroe	30D3/40A2
Carlton Colville	22E2	Chatburn	30D3/40A1		25A5/30G2/40D1	Clock Face	24A1/25A3/40E3
Carlton-on-Trent	27E4	Chatham	7B5/13G5	Christchurch	4E1/5F2	Clough Fold	30E2/40B1

Station	Ref	Station	Ref
Devonport (L&SW)	2E5	Drayton (Norfolk)	22C4
Devynock	16D3/17F3	Drayton (Sussex)	6E4
Dewsbury (GN)	31E2	Driffield	32C4
Dewsbury (L&NW)	31E2	Drigg	33F4
Dewsbury (L&Y)	31E2	Drighlington	31E1
Dicconson Lane	30F4/40C2	Droitwich	18C1
Didcot	12E5	Droitwich Road Goods	18D1/19G1
Didsbury	25A5/30G2/40E1	Dronfield	26B2/27D1
Digby	28F5	Droxford for Hambledon	5D5
Diggle	30F1	Droylsden	26A5/30G2
Dinas (FR)	23D4	Drumburgh	34A5
Dinas (TV)	9B5/16G2	Drws-y-Nant	23F5/19G4
Dinas Junction	23C3	Drybrook Road	10A1/18G3
Dinas Powis	10D5	Drypool Goods	28A5/32E3
Dingestow	10A2	Drysllwyn	16E5/17G1
Dinmore	18D4	Dudbridge	11D1
Dinsdale	35E5	Dudley (GW)	18B1/19D1
Dinting	26A5/30G1	Dudley (L&NW)	18B1
Dinton	4B2/5C1	Dudley Hill	31E1
Disley	26B5	Dudley Port (GW)	18A1/19D1
Diss	22F4	Dudley Port (L&NW)	18A1/19D1
Distinton	33D4	Duffield	19A4/26E2/27G1
Ditchford	20F3	Duffws	23D4
Ditchingham	22E3	Dukeries Junction	27E4
Ditton	24A1/25B2/40E3	Dukinfield	26A5
Dixonfold	25A5/30F2/40D1	Dullingham	21G3/13A4
Docking	21A4	Dulverton	3B1/9G5
Doddington & Harby	27E5	Dunball	3A4/10F3
Dodworth	26A2/27B1/31F2	Dunbridge	5C3
Doe Hill	26D2/27F2	Dunchurch	19F5
Dogdyke	28F4	Dunford Bridge	26A4/31G1
Dolau	16A1/17C5	Dungeness	8F4
Doldowlod	16A2/17B4	Dunham	21C5
Dolgoch	17A1/23G4	Dunham Hill	24B1/25C2/40F4
Dollgelley	23F4	Dunham Massey	25A4/40E2
Dolwen	17B4	Dunhampstead Goods	18D1/19G1
Dolwyddelen	23D5/19E3	Dunmow	13C4/39A5
Dolygaer	10A5/16E2/17G4	Duns	37B5
Dolyhir	16B1	Dunsland Cross	2B5
Dolywern	24E3	Dunstable (GN)	12C1/39A2
Doncaster	26A1/27C3/31F4	Dunstable (L&NW)	12C1/39A1
Doncaster Marsh Gate Goods	27C3/31F4	Dunstall Park	18A1
Donington Road	20A1	Dunster	3A2/9F5
Donington-on-Bain	28D4	Dunton Green	7C3/39F4
Donisthorpe	19C4/26G4	Dunvant	9B2/16F5
Donnington	25G4	Durham	35C4
Dorchester (GW)	4E4	Dursley	11E1
Dorchester (L&SW)	4E4	Durston	3B4/10G3
Dore & Totley	26B2/27D1	Dyffryn	23F3
Dorking (LB&SC)	6A2/39G2	Dymock	18F2
Dorking (SE&C)	6B2/39G2	Dynant	9A2
Dormans	7D2/39G4	Dynevor	9B3/16F4
Dornoch	33A5		
Dorrington	18A4/24G1	Eaglescliffe	35E5
Dorstone	18E5	Ealing (GW)	13F1/39D2
Doublebois	1E5	Ealing (Met & Dist)	13F1/39D2
Douglas	29F3	Earby	30C2
Dousland	2E4	Eardington	18B2
Dove Holes	26B4	Eardisley	18E5
Dovecliffe	26A2/27C1/31G3	Earith Bridge	21F1
Dover Harbour	8D2	Earlestown	24A1/25A3/30G4/40D3
Dover Pier	8D2	Earley	12G3
Dover Priory	8D2	Earlsfield	7B1/13G2/39E3
Dover Town	8D2	Earlston	37C4
Dovercourt	14C2	Earlswood	6B1/7C1/39G3
Dowlais (B&M)	10A5/16E2	Earsham	22E3
Dowlais (GW)	10A5/16E2	Earswick	31C4
Dowlais (TV)	10A5/16E2	Easington	36E4
Dowlais High Street	10A5/16E2	Easingwold	31B4
Dowlais Top	10A5/16E2	East Anstey	3B1/9G4
Downham	21D3	East Barkwith	28D4
Downton	4B1/5D2	East Boldon	35B5
Drax	27A3/31E5	East Budleigh	3E3
Draycott (Notts)	19A4/26F1	East Croydon	6A1/7B1/13G2/39F3
Draycott (Som)	3A5/10E2	East Farleigh	7C4
		East Finchley	13F2/39D3

Station	Ref	Station	Ref
East Garston	11F5	Elmers End	7B2/13G3/39E3
East Gate	21G5	Elmesthorpe	19D5
East Grinstead	7D2	Elmswell	22G5
East Horndon	7A4/13F4/39D5	Elmton & Creswell	26C1/27E2
East Langton	20D5	Elrington	35A1
East Leake	19B5/26F1	Elrington	34A1
East Margate	8B2/14G1	Elsecar & Hoyland	26A2/27C1/31G3
East Minster-on-Sea	8B5/14G4	Elsenham	13C4/39A5
East Norton	20D4	Elsham	28B5/32F4
East Rosedale Goods	36F4	Elslack	30C1
East Rudham	21B5	Elsted	6D4
East Southsea	5E5	Elstree	13E1/39C2
East Ville	28F3	Elswick	35A4
East Winch	21C4	Eltham	7B2/13G3/39E4
Eastbourne	7G4	Elton (GN)	20A2/27G4
Eastbury	11F5	Elton (L&NW)	20D2
Eastchurch	8B5/14G4	Elvet	35C4
Eastgate	34C1/35C2	Ely (GW)	10C5
Eastleigh & Bishopstoke	5D4	Ely Main Line	10C5
Eastoft	27B4/32E5	Ely (Cambs)	21F2
Easton Lodge	13C4/39B5	Embleton	33D5
Easton	4F4	Embsay	30C1
Easton Court	18C3	Emneth	21D2
Eastrington (HB&W)	27A4/32E5	Emsworth	6E5
Eastrington (NE)	27A4/32E5	Enderby	19D5
Eastwood	30E1	Endon	26D5
Eastwood Road	26E1	Enfield Lock	13E3/39C3
Eaton	18B5	Enfield (GE)	13E2/39C3
Ebberston	32A5	Enfield (GN)	13E2/39C3
Ebbw Vale (GW)	10A4/16E1	Enthorpe	32C5
Ebbw Vale (L&NW)	10A4/16E1	Entwistle	30E3/40C2
Ebchester	35B3	Epping	13E3/39C4
Ebdon Lane	10D3	Epsom (L&SW)	6A2/7C1/39F2
Ecclefechan	37G1	Epsom (LBSC)	6A2/7C1/39F2
Eccles	25A5/30G2/40D1	Epsom Downs	6A2/7B1/39F2
Eccles Road	22E5	Epworth	27C4/31F
Ecclesfield (GC)	26A2/27C1/31G3	Erdington	19D2
Ecclesfield (Mid)	26A2/27C1/31G2	Eridge	7D3
Eccleshill	31D1	Erith	7A3/13F4/39E4
Eccleston Park	24A1/25A2/30G5/40E4	Erwood	16C2/17E5
Eckington & Renishaw (GC)	26B1/27D2	Eryholme	35F4
Eckington & Renishaw (Mid)	26B1/27D2	Escrick	31D4
Eckington	11B2/18E1	Esgairgeiliog	17A2/23G5
Ecton	26D4	Esher & Claremont	13G1/39F2
Edale	26B4	Esholt	31D1
Eden Park	7B2/13G3/39D3	Eskdale Green	33F5
Edenbridge	7C2/39G4	Eskett	33E4
Edenbridge Town	7D2/39G4	Eskmeals	33F4
Edge Hill	24A2/25B2/40E4	Essendine	20C2
Edgware	13D1/39D2	Eston	36E5
Edlingham	38E3	Etchingham	7E4
Edlington	21G2	Etherley	35D3
Edmondthorpe & Wymondham	20B4	Etruria	25E5
Edrom	38A5	Ettingshall Road & Bilston	18A1/19D1
Edwalton	20A5	Ettington	11A4
Edwinstowe	27D3	Etwall	19B3/26F3
Efail Isaf	10C5/16G2	Euxton	30E4/40C3
Effingham Junction	6A2/39F1	Evenwood	35D3
Eggesford	2A3	Evercreech Junction	4A5/10F1
Egginton	19B3/26F3	Evercreech New	4A4/10F1
Egham	39E1	Everingham	32D5
Egloskerry	1C5	Evershot	4D5
Egremont	33E4	Evesham (GW)	11A3
Egton	36F3	Evesham (Mid)	11A3
Elburton Cross	2F4	Ewell (L&SW)	6A2/7B1/39F2
Elham	8D3	Ewell (LB&SC)	6A2/7B1/39F2
Elland	31E1/42C1	Ewesley	38F4
Ellenbrook	25A4/30G3/40D2	Ewood Bridge	30E2/40C1
Ellesmere	24E2/25F2	Exeter Queen Street	2C1/3E1
Ellesmere Port	24B2/25C2/40F4	Exeter St Davids	2C1/3E1
Ellingham	22E3	Exeter St Thomas	2C1/3E1
Elmbridge	21D2	Exminster	2C1/3E2
		Exmouth	2D1
		Eyarth	24C4

Station	Reference
Kershope Foot	37G3
Keswick	34D5
Ketley	25G4
Kettering	20E4
Kettleness	36E3
Kew Bridge	7A1/13F1/39E2
Kew Gardens	29F5/40C4/39D3
Keyham	2E5
Keyingham	28A432E2
Keynsham	10D1
Kibworth	20D5
Kidbrooke	7A2/13G3/39E4
Kidderminster	18C1
Kidlington	12C5
Kidsgrove	25D5/40G1
Kidwelly	9A1/15F5
Kielder	37F4
Kilburn	26E2/27G1
Kildale	36E5
Kildwick & Crosshills	30C1
Kilgerran	15C3
Kilgetty	15F3
Killamarsh (GC)	26B1/27D2
Killamarsh (Mid)	26B1/27D2
Killay	9B2/16G5
Killingworth	35A4/38G2
Killywhan	33A3
Kilnhurst (GC)	26A1/27C2/31G3
Kilnhurst (Mid)	26A1/27C2/31G3
Kilnwick Gate Goods	32C4
Kimberley	22D5
Kimberley (GN)	19A5/26E1/27G2
Kimberley (Mid)	19A5/26E1/27G2
Kimbolton	20F2
Kincraig	36G4
Kineton	11A5/19G4
King William	30F3/40C2
King's Heath	19E2
King's Langley	12D1/39G1
King's Norton	19E2
King's Sutton	12B5
Kingsbridge	2F3
Kingsbury (Mid)	19D3
Kingsbury (London)	7A1/13F1/39D2
Kingscliffe	20D2
Kingscote	7D2
Kingskerswell	2E2/3F1
Kingsland	18D4
Kingston Road	10D3
Kingston (Surrey)	13G1/39E2
Kingston (Sussex)	6E1/7G1
Kingswear	2F2
Kingswood & Burgh Heath	6A1/7C1/39F3
Kington	18D5
Kinnersley	18E5
Kinnerton	24C2/25D1/40G5
Kintbury	11G5
Kipling Cotes	32D4
Kippax	27A1/31E3
Kirby Cross	14C3
Kirby Moorside	36G4
Kirby Muxloe	19D5
Kirby Park	24A1/25B1/40E5
Kirk Smeaton	27B2/31F4
Kirkandrews	34A5
Kirkbank	37C5
Kirkbride	33B5
Kirkburton	31F1
Kirkby	29A5/33G5/30G5/40D4
Kirkby Lonsdale	30D4
Kirkby Stephen	34E2
Kirkby Stephen & Ravenstonedale	34E2
Kirkby Thore	34D3
Kirkby-in-Ashfield (GC)	26D1/27F2
Kirkby-in-Ashfield (Mid)	26D1/27F2
Kirkcudbright	33B1
Kirkgunzeon	33A3
Kirkham	30D5/40B4
Kirkham Abbey	31B5
Kirkheaton	31F1
Kirklington	27F3
Kirkmichael	29E2
Kirknewton	38C5
Kirkpatrick	34A5
Kirkstall	31D2
Kirkstall Forge	31D2
Kirkstead	28F4
Kirtlebridge	33A5/37G1
Kirton	21A1/28G2
Kirton Lindsey	27C5/32G4
Kiveton Park	26B1/27D2
Knapton	32A5
Knaresborough	31C2
Knebworth	13C2/39B3
Knighton	18C5
Knightwick	18D2
Knitsley	35B3
Knockholt	7B3/39F4
Knottingley	27A2/31E3
Knotty Ash	24A2/25A2/40E4
Knowesgate	38F4
Knowle & Dorridge	19F2
Knutsford	25B4/40F2
Ladmanlow	26C5
Laindon	7A4/13F5
Laisterdyke	31D1
Lakenheath	21E4
Lambley	34B2
Lambourn	11F5
Lamesley	35B4
Lampeter	17E1/16C5
Lamphey	15F2
Lamplugh	33D4
Lamport	20F4
Lancaster Castle	30B5
Lancaster Green Ayre	30B5
Lanchester	35C3
Lancing	6E2
Landore	9B3/16F5
Langford (Beds)	13B1
Langford (Essex)	14D5
Langford (Som)	10E2
Langho	30D3/40A2
Langley (Bucks)	12F1/39E1
Langley (Northumb)	34A1/35B1
Langley Green	19D1
Langley Mill Goods	26E1/27G2
Langolm	37F2
Langport (East)	3B5/10G3
Langport (West)	3B5/10G3
Langrick	28G4
Langstone	6E5
Langwathby	34C3
Langwith	26C1/27E2
Langworth	28E5
Lapford	2B3
Lapworth	19F3
Lartington	35E2
Latchford	25B3
Launceston (GW)	1C5
Launceston (L&SW)	1C5
Launton	12C4
Lavant	6D4
Lavenham	14A5
Lavernock	10D4
Lavington	5A1
Lawrence Hill	10D1
Lawton	25D5/40G1
Laxey	29F3
Laxfield	22F3
Lazonby & Kirkoswald	34C3
Lea	27D5
Lea Bridge	7A2/13F3/39D3
Lea Green	24A1/25A3/30G4/40E3
Lea Road	30D5
Leadenham	27F5
Leadgate	35B3
Leagrave	12C1/39A1
Lealholm	36F4
Leamington (GW)	19F4
Leamington (L&NW)	19F4
Leamside	35C4
Leasowe	24A3/25A1/40E5
Leatherhead (L&SW)	6A2/39F2
Leatherhead (LB&SC)	6A2/39F2
Leaton	24F1/25G2
Lechlade	11D4
Leckhampton	11C2/18G1
Ledbury	18E2
Ledsham	24B2/25C1/40F4
Ledstone	27A2/31E3
Lee	7B2/13G3/39E4
Leebotwood	18A4
Leeds Central	31D2
Leeds Marsh Lane	31D2
Leeds New	31D2
Leeds Wellington	31D2
Leegate	33C5
Lee-on-the-Solent	5E5
Leek	26D5
Leeming Bar	35G4
Legacy	24D2/25E1
Legbourne Road	28D3
Leicester (GC)	19C5
Leicester (GN)	20C5
Leicester (L&NW Goods)	20C5
Leicester (Mid)	20D5
Leicester West Bridge	19C5
Leigh & Bedford	25A4/30G3/40D2
Leigh (Essex)	7A5/14F5
Leigh (Lancs)	20B2/24F2/45C3
Leigh (Staffs)	19A1
Leigh Court	11A1/18D2
Leigh's Wood	19D2
Leighton	12C2
Leiston	22G2
Lelant	1A2
Lemington	35A3
Lenham	8C5
Lenton	19A5/26E1/27G3
Lenwade	22C4
Leominster	18D4
Letterston	15D1
Levenshulme (GC)	25A5/30E2/40D1
Levenshulme (L&NW)	25A5/30G2/40D1
Leverton	27D4
Levisham	36G3
Lewes	7F2
Leyburn	35G3
Leycett	25G5
Leyland	30E4/40B3
Leysdown	8B4/14G4
Leyton	7A2/13F3/39D4
Leytonstone	7A2/13F3/39D4
Lezayre	29E3
Lichfield City	19C2
Lichfield Trent Valley High Level	19C2/26G4
Lichfield Trent Valley Low Level	19C2/26G4
Lidlington	12B1
Lifford	19E2
Lifton	2C5
Lightcliffe	31E1
Lightmoor	18A3
Lilbourne	19E5
Limpley Stoke	11G1
Linby (GN)	26D1/27F2
Linby (Mid)	26D1/27F2
Lincoln (GN)	27E5
Lincoln (Mid)	27E5
Lindal	29A5
Linefoot	33C4
Lingfield	7D2/39G4
Lingwood	22D3
Linley	18A2
Linton	13A4
Lintz Green	35B3
Liphook	6C4
Liscard	24A2/25A1/40E5
Liskeard	1E5
Liss	6C5
Litchfield	5A4
Little Bytham	20C2
Little Eaton	19A4/26E2/27G1
Little Hulton	25A4/30F3/40D2
Little Kimble	12D3
Little Mill	38D3
Little Mill Junction	10B3
Little Salkeld	34C3
Little Somerford	11F2
Little Steeping	28F2
Little Sutton	24B2/25B2/40F4
Little Weighton	32D4
Littleborough	30F1
Littleham	2D1/3E2
Littlehampton	6E3
Littlemore	12D5
Littleport	21E3
Littleton & Badsey	11A3
Littleworth	20C1
Liverpool Central	24A2/25B1/40E4
Liverpool Exchange	24A2/25B1/40E4
Liverpool Lime Street	24A2/25B1/40E4
Liverpool St James	24A2/25B1/40E4
Liversedge Central	31E1
Llanarthney	17G1
Llanbadarn	17B1
Llanbedr & Pensarn	23E3
Llanberis (L&NW)	23C3
Llanberis (SMR)	23C3
Llanbister Road	17C5/16A4
Llanbradach	10B5/16G1
Llanbrynmair	17A3/24G5
Llancaiach	10B5
Llandaff	10C5/3B4
Llandebie	9A3/16E5/17G1
Llandenny	10A3
Llanderfel	24E5
Llandilo	16D5/17G1
Llandilo Bridge	16D5/17G1
Llandinam	17B4
Llandovery	16D4/1752
Llandrillo	24E4
Llandrindod Wells	16B2/17D4
Llandudno Juntion	23B5
Llandudno	23B5
Llandulas	24B5
Llandyssil	15C5
Llanelly	9B2/15F5
Llanelly Docks	9B2
Llanerchymedd	23A2
Llanfair	23B3
Llanfair Caereinion	17A5/24G4
Llanfairfechan	23B4

Station	Reference
Meir	19A1
Melangoose Mill	1E3
Melbourne	19B4/26F2
Meldreth & Melbourn	13B3
Melksham	11F2
Melling	30B4
Mellis	22F5
Mells Road	10E1
Melmerby	31A2
Melrose	37C3
Meltham	31F1
Melton Constable	22B5
Melton Mowbray (GN & L&NW)	20B4
Melton Mowbray (Mid)	20B4
Melton	14A2
Menai Bridge	23B3
Mendlesham	22G4
Menheniot	1E5
Menston	31D1
Menthorpe Gate	31D5
Meols	24A3/25B1/40E5
Meols Cop	40C4
Meopham	7B4/13G5/39E5
Mersey Road	24A2/25B2/40E4
Merstham	6A1/7C1/39F3
Merstone	5F5
Merthyr	10A5
Merthyr High Street	10A5
Merthyr Vale	10B5/16F2
Merton Park	7B1/13E2/39E3
Methley (L&Y)	27A1/31E3
Methley (Mid)	27A1/31E3
Mexborough	26A1/27C2/31G3
Micheldever	5B5
Mickle Trafford (Birkenhead Jt)	24B1/25C2/40F4
Mickle Trafford (CLC)	24B1/25C2/40F4
Micklefield	31D3
Micklehurst	26A5/30G1
Mickleover	19A3/26E3
Mickleton	35D2
Middle Drove	21C2
Middlesbrough	36E5
Middleton Town	30F2/40D1
Middleton Junction	25A5/30F2/40D1
Middleton (Norfolk)	21C3
Middleton (Northumb)	38F4
Middleton (Shropshire)	18C4
Middleton (Westm)	34G3
Middleton-in-Teesdale	34D1/35D2
Middleton-on-the-Wolds	32C4
Middletown	24G3/25G1
Middlewich	25C4/40F2
Middlewood (Macc Ctee)	26B5
Middlewood (Mid)	26B5
Midge Hall	30E4/40B5
Midgham	12G4
Midhurst (LB&SC)	6D4
Midhurst	6D4
Midsomer Norton & Welton	10E1
Milborne Port	4C4
Milcote	11A4/19G3
Mildenhall	21F4
Miles Platting	25A5/30G2/40D1
Milford Junction	27A2/31E3
Milford & Brocton	19B1/26G5
Milford	6B3
Mill Street	9A5
Mill Hill (GN)	13E2/39D2
Mill Hill (IoW)	5E4
Mill Hill (Lancs)	30E3/40B2
Mill Hill (Mid)	13E1/39D2
Millbay	2F5
Millbrook (Beds)	12B1
Millbrook (Hants)	5D4
Miller's Dale	26C4
Millfield	35B5
Millhouses	26B2/27D1
Millom	29A4/33G5
Milnrow	30F1
Milnthorpe	30A4/34G4
Milton Road	10D3
Milverton	3B3/10G5
Mindrum	38C5
Minehead	3A2/9F5
Minera Lime Works	24D3/25D1
Minety	11E3
Minffordd (Cam)	23E3
Minffordd (FR)	23E3
Minshull Vernon	25D4/40G2
Minster (Kent)	8B2/14G2
Minster (Sheppey)	8B5/14G4
Minsterley	24G2
Mirfield	31E1
Misterton	27C4/31G5
Mistley	14C3
Mitcham	7B1/13G2/39E3
Mitcham Junction	7B1/13G2/39E3
Mitcheldean Road	18G3
Moat Lane Junction	17B4
Mobberley	40E1
Mochdre & Pabo	23B5
Moira	19C4/26G2
Mold	24C3/40G5
Mollington	24B2/40F4
Molyneux Brow	25A5/30F2/40D1
Monk Bretton	27B1/31F3
Monkseaton	35A5/38G2
Monmore Green	18A1/19D1
Monmouth May Hill	10A2/18G4
Monmouth Troy	10A2/18G4
Monsal Dale	26C3
Montacute	4C5
Montgomery	17A5
Monton Green	25A4/30G3/40D1
Montpelier	10D1
Monument Lane	19E2
Moor Row	33E4
Moor End Goods	26A3/27C1/31/G2
Moore	25B3/40E3
Moorhampton	18E5
Moorhouse	27B2/31F3
Moorside	25A4/30G3/40D1
Moorswater	1E5
Moorthorpe & South Kirkby	27B2/31F3
Moortown	28C5/32G3
Morchard Road	2B3
Morcott	20D3
Morden	7B1/13G2/39E3
Morebath	3B2/9G5
Morecambe (L&NW)	30B5
Morecambe	30B5
Morecambe Pier	30B5
Moresby Parks	33D4
Moreton (Dorset)	4E3
Moreton (Wirral)	24A3/25A1/40E5
Moretonhampstead	2C3
Moreton-in-Marsh	11B4
Moreton-on-Lugg	18E4
Morley (GN)	31E2
Morley (L&NW)	31E2
Morpeth	38F3
Morriston	9B3/16F5
Mortehoe	9F2
Mortimer	12G4
Mortlake	7A1/13G1/39E2
Morton Pinkney	12A4
Morton Road	20B2
Moseley	19E2
Moses Gate	30F3
Mosley Street	19B3/26F3
Moss	27B3/31F4
Moss & Pentre	24D2/25D1
Moss Bank	24A1/25A3/40D3
Moss Bridge	29F5/40C5
Moss Side	30E5/40B4
Mossley	26A5/30G1
Mossley Hill	24A2/25B2/40E4
Moston	25A5/30G2/40D1
Mostyn	24B4
Mottisfont	5C3
Mottram & Broadbottom	26A5/27G1
Mouldsworth	24B1/25C3/40F3
Moulton (Lincs)	21C1)
Moulton (Yorks)	35F4
Mountain Ash (GW)	10B5/16F2
Mountain Ash (TV)	10B5/16F2
Mow Cop	25D5/40G1
Much Wenlock	18A3
Mumbles	9C2/16G5
Mumbles Road (L&NW)	9B3/16G5
Mumbles Road (S&M)	9B3/16G5
Mumby Road	28E2
Muncaster	33F4
Mundesley-on-Sea	22B3
Murrow (GN & GE)	21D1
Murrow (M&GN)	21D1
Murton	35C5
Musgrave	34E2
Muswell Hill	13F2/39D3
Mutley	2E5
Mynydd y Garreg Goods	9A1/15E5
Mytholmroyd	30E1
Naburn	31C4
Nafferton	32B4
Nailsea	10D2
Nailsworth	11E1
Nancegollan	1B2
Nannerch	24C3
Nantclwyd	24D4
Nantgaredig	15D5
Nantlle	23D3
Nantmawr	24F3/25F1
Nantwich	25D4/24E2
Nantybwch	10A5/16E1
Nantyderry	10A3
Nantyffyllon	9B4/16F3
Nantyglo	10A4/16E1
Nantymoel	9B5/16F3
Nantyronen	17C2
Napton & Stockton	19F5
Narberth	15E3
Narborough (GE)	21C4
Narborough (L&NW)	19D5
Nassington	20D2
Nateby	30C5
Naworth	34A3
Nawton	31A5/36G4
Neath (GW)	9B4/16F4
Neath (N&B)	9B4/16F4
Neath (RS&B)	9B4/16F4
Neath Abbey	9B3/16F4
Needham	14A3
Neen Sollars	18C3
Neepsend	26B2/27D1
Nelson (L&Y)	30D2/40A1
Nelson (TV)	10B5/16F1
Neptune Street Goods	28A5/32E3
Neston (Birkenhead Jt)	24B2/25B1/40F2
Neston (N.Wales & L'pool)	24B2/25B1
Netherfield	19A5/27G3
Netherton (GW)	18B1/19E1
Netherton (L&Y)	31F1
Nethertown	33E4
Netley	5D4
New Barnet	13E2/39C3
New Basford	19A1/26E1/27G3
New Biggin	34D3
New Bridge	35A4
New Brighton	24A2/25A1/29G5/40D5
New Brompton	7B5
New Clee	28B3/32F2
New Eltham	7B2/13G3/39E4
New Galloway	33A1
New Hey	30F1
New Holland	28A5/32E3
New Holland Pier	28A5/32E3
New Lane	30FF5/40C4
New Milford	15F2
New Mills (L&NW)	26B5
New Mills (S&M)	26B5
New Milton	5E2
New Quay Road	15C5
New Radnor	16B1
New Romney & Littlestone-on-Sea	8E4
New Southgate	13E2/39D3
New Tredegar	16F1
Newark (GN)	27F4
Newark (Mid)	27F4
Newbiggin-by-the-Sea	38F2
Newbridge	10B4/16F1
Newbridge-on-Wye	16B2/17D4
Newburn	35A3
Newbury	12G5
Newby Wiske	35G5
Newcastle Central	35A4
Newcastle Emlyn	15C4
Newcastle under Lyme	25E5/24F1
Newcastleton	37F3
Newchurch	5F5
Newent	18F2
Newham	38C3
Newhaven Harbour	7G2
Newhaven Town	7G2
Newick & Chailey	7E2
Newington	7B5/14G5
Newland	10A2/18G3
Newlay	31D2
Newlyn East	1F2
Newmarket	21G3
Newnham	10A1/18G3
Newnham Bridge	18C3
Newport Mill Street Goods	10C3
Newport (Essex)	13B4/39A5
Newport (IoW)	5F4
Newport (Shrops)	25G4
Newport (Yorks)	27A5/32D5
Newport Alexandra Docks	10C3
Newport Dock Street	10C3
Newport High Street	10C343A3
Newport Pagnell	12A2
Newquay	1E2
Newquay Harbour	1E2
Newsham	28A5
Newsholme	30C2
Newstead (GN)	26D1/27F2
Newstead (Mid)	26D1/27F2
Newthorpe	19A5/26E1
Newton	26A5/30G1
Newton Abbot	2D2/3F1
Newton Heath	25A5/30G2/40D1
Newton Kyme	31D3

Place	Ref
Newton Road	19D1
Newton Tony	5B2
Newton-le-Willows	25A3/30G4/40D3
Newtown	17B5
Nidd Bridge	31B2
Nine Mile Point	10B4/16G1
Ningwood	5F4
Nisbet	37D4
Nocton & Dunston	28F5/17B1
Norbiton	7B1/13G1/39E2
Norbury	19A2/26E4
Norham	38B5
Normacot	19A1/26E5
Normanton	27A1/31E3
North Blyth	38F2
North Bridge	31E1
North Camp (L&SW)	6E4
North Camp (S&EC)	6E4
North Cave	32D5
North Dock (Sunderland)	35B5
North Drove	20B1
North Elmham	22C5
North Grimston	32B5
North Hayling	6E5
North Kelsey	28C5/32G3
North Lonsdale Crossing Halt	34G5
North Mersey	24A2/25A1/29G5/40D5
North Seaton	38F2
North Shields	35A5
North Sunderland	38C3
North Tawton	2B3
North Thoresby	28C3/32G2
North Walsall	19D1
North Walsham (GE)	22B3
North Walsham (M&GN)	22B3
North Weald	13E4/39C4
North Woolwich	7A2/13F3/39E4
North Wootton	21B3
North Wylam	35A3
Northallerton	35G5
Northallerton Town	35F5
Northam (Devon)	9G1
Northam (Hants)	5D4
Northampton (Mid)	20G4
Northampton Bridge Street	20G4
Northampton Castle	20G4
Northenden	25B5/40E1
Northfield	19E1
Northfleet	7B4/13G4/39E5
Northiam	7E5
Northorpe (GC)	27C5/32G5
Northorpe (L&Y)	31E1
Northwich	25C4/40F2
Northwood	12E1/13E1/39D1
Norton (L&NW)	25A3/40E3
Norton (L&Y)	27B2/31F4
Norton Bridge (L&NW)	25F5
Norton Bridge (NS)	25F5
Norton Fitzwarren	3B3/10G4
Norton Junction	11A2/18D1
Norton-in-Hales	25E4/24C2
Norton-on-Tees	35D5
Norwich City	22D4
Norwich Thorpe	22D4
Norwich Victoria	22D4
Norwood Junction	7B2/13G2/39E3
Nostell	27B1/31F3
Notgrove	11C3
Nottingham (L&NW Goods)	19A5/27G3
Nottingham Arkwright Street	19A5/27G3
Nottingham London Rd Low Level	19A5/27G3
Nottingham (Mid)	19A5/26E1/27G3
Nottingham Victoria	19A5/26E1/27G3
Notton & Royston	27B1/31F2
Nunburnholme	32C5
Nuneaton (L&NW)	19D4
Nuneaton (Mid)	19D4
Nunnington	31A5
Nunthorpe	36E5
Nursling	5D3
Nutfield	6B1/7C1/39G3
Oakamoor	19A2/26E4
Oakengates (GW)	25G4
Oakengates (L&NW)	25G4
Oakenshaw	27A1/31E3
Oakham	20C4
Oakington	21G2
Oakle Street	11C1/18G2
Oakleigh Park	13E2/39C3
Oakley (Beds)	12A1/20G2
Oakley (Hants)	5A5
Oakworth	30D1
Oatlands	33D4
Ockendon	7A3/13F4
Ocker Hill	18A1/19D1
Ockley & Capel	6B2
Offord & Buckden	20F1
Ogbourne	11F4
Ogmore Vale	9B5/16G3
Okehampton	2C4
Old Colwyn	24B5
Old Dalby	20B5
Old Hill	19E1
Old Leake	28F3
Old Milford	15F1
Old North Road	13A2
Old Trafford	25A5/30G2/40D1
Old Woods Goods	24F1/25G2
Oldbury	19E1
Oldbury & Bromford Lane	19E1
Oldbury & Langley Green	19E1
Oldham Central	30F1
Oldham Clegg Street	26A5/30F1
Oldham Glodwick Road	30F1
Oldham Mumps	30F1
Oldham Werneth	30F2
Ollerton	27E3
Olney	12A2/20G3
Olton	19E2
Ongar	13E4/39C5
Onibury	18B4
Onllwyn	9A4/16E3
Ordsall Lane	25A5/30G2/40D1
Ore	7F5
Ormesby	36E5
Ormside	34D2
Ormskirk	30F5/40C4
Orpington	7B2/13G3/39F4
Orrell	25A3/30F4/40D3
Orwell	14B2
Ossett	31E2
Osterley	13F1/39E2
Oswestry (Cam)	24E2/25F1
Oswestry GW	24E2/25F1
Otford	7C3/39F5
Otley	31D1
Otterham	1C4
Otterington	35G5
Otterspool	24A2/25B2/40E4
Ottery St Mary	3E3
Ottringham	28A4/32E2
Oughty Bridge	26A2/27C1/31G2
Oulton Broad	22E1
Oundle	20E2
Outwell Basin	21D2
Outwell Village	21D2
Over & Wharton	25C4/40F2
Overseal & Moira	19C3/26G3
Overton	20D1
Overton-on-Dee	24E2/25E2
Oxenholme	34F4
Oxenhope	30D1
Oxford (GW)	12D5
Oxford (L&NW)	12D5
Oxheys Goods	30E4
Oxshott for Fairmile	6A2/39F2
Oxted	7C2/39F4
Padbury	12B3
Paddock Wood	7D4
Padeswood	24C3/25D1/40G5
Padgate	25B3/40E2/45C4
Padiham	30D2/40B1
Padstow	1D3
Paignton	2E2/3G1
Palace Gates	13E2/39D3
Pallion	35B5
Palmers Green	13E2/39D3
Palteron & Sutton	26C1/27E2
Pampisford	13A4
Pandy	18F5
Pangbourne	12F4
Pannal	31C2
Pant Glas	23D3
Pant (Cam)	24F3/25F1
Pant (B&M)	10A5/16E2
Pantydwr	16A2/17C4
Pantyffynnon	9A3/16E5
Papcastle	33D4
Par	1F4
Parbold	30F5/40C3
Parham	22G3
Park (Furness)	29A4
Park (GE)	13E2/39D3
Park Bridge	26A5/30G1
Park Drain	27C4/31G5
Park Street & Frogmore	13D1/39C2
Parkend	10A1
Parkeston Quay	14B2
Parkgate(Birkenhead Jt)	24B3/25B1/40F5
Parkgate (Yorks)	26A2/27C1/31G3
Parkgate & Akdwarke	26A1/27C2/31G3
Parkhead Goods	35C2
Parkstone	4E2/5F1
Parsley Hay	26C4
Partington	25A4/28A3/30G3/40E2
Parton (Cumb)	33D3
Parton (Kirkud)	33A1
Partridge Green	6D2
Paston & Knapton	22B3
Patchway & Stoke Gifford	10C1
Pateley Bridge	31B1
Patney & Chirton	5A1
Patricroft	25A5/30G2/40D1
Patrington	32E2
Peak Forest	26C4
Peakirk	20C1
Peartree & Normanton	19A4/26F2
Peasley Cross	24A1/25A3/40D3
Peckham Rye	7A2/13G3/39E3
Pedair-Ffordd	24F4
Peel	29F2
Peel Road	29F2
Pegswood	38F3
Pelaw	35B4
Pelton	35B4
Pemberton	25A3/30F4/40D3
Pembrey & Burry Port	9B1/15F5
Pembroke Dock	15F2
Pembroke Town	15F2
Penally	15F3
Penarth	10D4
Penarth Dock	10D4
Pencader	15C5
Penclawdd	9B2
Pencoed	9C5/16G3
Pendlebury	25A5/30G2/40D1
Pendleton	25A5/30G2/40D1
Pendre	17A1
Pengam (B&M)	10B5/16F1
Pengam (Rhymney)	10B5/16F1
Penistone	26A3/31G2
Penkridge	19C1/26G5
Penmaenmawr	23B4
Penmaenpool	23F4
Pennard	4A5/10F2
Pennington	25A4/30G3/40D2
Penns	19D2
Penpergwm	10A3
Penrhiwceiber	10B5/16F2
Penrhyn	23E4
Penrhyndeudraeth	23E4
Penrith	34D4
Penruddock	34D4
Penryn	1G2
Pensford	10D1
Penshaw	35B4
Penshurst	7D3/39G5
Pentewan	1F3
Penton	37G3
Pentrebach	10A5/16F2
Pentrefelin	24F3
Penwyllt	9A4/16E3/17G3
Penybont	16A2/17D5
Penybontfawr	24F4
Penyffordd	24C2/25D1/40G5
Penygraig	9B5/16G2
Penygroes	23D3
Penyrheol Junction	10C5/16G1
Penzance	1B1
Peplow	25F3
Percy Main	35A5
Perranporth	1F2
Perranwell	1G2
Perry Barr	19D2
Pershore	11A2/18E1
Peterborough (GE)	20D1
Peterborough (GN)	20D1
Peterchurch	18E5
Petersfield	6C5
Peterston	10C5
Petworth	6D3
Pevensey & Westham	7G4
Pewsey	5A2/11G4
Pickburn	27B2/31F4
Pickering	32A5/36G3
Pickhill	35E5
Picton	35E5
Piddington	12A2/20G4
Piel	29B5
Piercebridge	35E4
Pill	10C2
Pilley Goods	26A2/27C1/31G2
Pilling	30C5/40A4
Pilmoor	31A3
Pilning	10C2
Pilsley	26D2/27F2
Pinchbeck	20B1
Pinchingthorpe	36E5
Pinhoe	2C1/3E2

Station	Ref
Pinner	13F1/39D2
Pinner & Hatch End	13E1/39D2
Pinxton (GN)	26D1/27F2
Pinxton (Mid)	26D1/27F2
Pipe Gate	25E4/24F2
Pitsea	7A5/13F5
Pitsford & Brampton	20F4
Pittington	35C4
Pitts Hll	25D5
Plas Power	24D2/25D1
Plas Marl	9B3/16F5
Plashetts	37F4
Plawsworth	35C4
Plealey Road	24G2
Pleasington	30E3/40B2
Pleasley	26C1/27E2
Plessey	38G2
Plocton	35E1
Plodder Lane	30F3/40D2
Plowden	18B5
Pluckley	8D5
Plumbley	25C4/40F2
Plumpton (Cumb)	34C4
Plumpton (Sussex)	6D1/7F2
Plumstead	7A2/13F3/39E4
Plumtree	20A5
Plymouth Friary	2F5
Plymouth North Road Jnc	2E5
Plympton	2E4
Plymstock	2F4
Pocklington	32C5
Pokesdown	4E4/5F2
Polegate	7G3
Polesworth	19D3
Polsham	10F2
Ponders End	13E3/39C3
Pont Fadog	24E3/25E1
Pont Llanio	17D1/16B5
Pont Rhydyfen	9B4/16F4
Pont Rhydyrun	10B4
Pont Rug	23C3
Pont Sarn	10A5/16E2
Pont Yeats	9A2/15E5
Pontardawe	9A3/16F4
Pontardulais (GW)	9A2/16F4
Pontardulais (L&NW)	9A2/16F4
Pontdolgoch	17A4
Pontefract	27A2/31E3
Pontefract Joint	27A2/31E3
Pontefract Tanshelf	27A2/31E3
Ponteland	35A3/38G3
Pontesbury	24G2
Pontfaen	24E3/25E1
Ponthir	10B3
Pontlottyn	10B5/16F1
Pontnewydd	10B4
Pontrhythallt	23C3
Pontrilas	18F5
Pontsticill	10A5/17G4
Pontyberem	9A2/15E5
Pontycymmer	9B5/16G3
Pont-y-Pant	23D5
Pontypool	10B4
Pontypool Crane Street	10B4
Pontypool Road	10B4
Pontypridd (Barry)	10B5/16G2
Pontypridd (TV)	10B5/16G2
Pontyrhyll	9B5/16G3
Pool	31D2
Pool Quay	24G3/25G1
Poole	4E2/5F1
Poppleton	31C4
Port Carlisle	33A5
Port Clarence	36D5
Port Dinorwic	23C3
Port Erin	29G1
Port Isaac Road	1D4
Port Penrhyn	23B3
Port Soderick	29F3
Port St Mary	29G2
Port Talbot (GW)	9B4/16G4
Port Talbot (Port Talbot)	9B4/16G4
Port Talbot (R&SB)	9B4/16G4
Port Talbot Dock	9B4/16G4
Port Victoria	7B5/8B5/14G5
Portbury	10C2
Portchester	5E5
Portesham	4E5
Porth	10B5/16G2
Porth Cawl	9C4
Porthywaen	24F3/25F1
Portishead	10C2
Portland	4F4
Portmadoc (Cam)	23E3
Portmadoc (FR)	23E3
Porton	4A4/5C2
Portreath	1F1
Portskewett	10C2
Portslade	6E1/7F1
Portsmouth Arms	2A3
Portsmouth Harbour	5E5
Portsmouth Town	5E5
Portsmouth (Yorks)	30E2
Postland	21C1
Potter Heigham	22B2
Potterhanworth	28E5
Potters Bar	13E2/39C3
Potto	35F5
Potton	13A2
Poulton	40A4
Powerstock	4D5
Poynto (Macc Ctee)	26B5
Poynton (L&NW)	26B5
Praze	1A2
Prees	24E1/25F3
Preesgweene	24E2/25E1
Prescot	24A1/25A2/30G5
Prestatyn	24B4
Prestbury	25B5
Presteign	18C5
Presthope	18A3
Preston (WL)	30E4/40B3
Preston Brook	25B3/40E3/45D5
Preston Joint	30E4/40B3
Preston Junction	30E4/40B3
Preston Park	6E1/7F1
Preston Road	24A2/25A2/29G5/40D4
Prestwich	25A5/30F2/40D
Priestfield	18A1/19D1
Princes End	18A1/19D1
Princes Risborough	12D3
Princetown	2D4
Prittlewell	8A5/14F5
Privett (LeeoS)	5E5
Privett (L&SW)	6C5
Prudhoe	35A3
Pudsey Greenside	31D1
Pudsey Lowtown	31D1
Pulborough	6D3
Pulford Goods	24C2/25D2/40G4
Pulham Market	22E4
Pulham St Mary	22E4
Puncheston	15D2
Purfleet	7A3/13F4/39E5
Purley	6A1/7B1/39F3
Purley Oaks	6A1/7B1/39F3
Purton	11E3
Putney	2A1/13G2/39E2
Putney Bridge	2A1/13G2/39E2
Puxton	10D3
Pwllheli	23E2
Pye Bridge	26D2/27F2
Pye Hill	26D1/27F2
Pyle	9C4/16G3
Pylle	4A5/10F1
Quainton Road	12C3
Quakers Drove	21E1
Quakers Yard High Level	10B5/16F2
Quakers Yard Low Level	10B5/16F2
Queenborough	8B5/14G5
Queens Ferry	24C2/25C1/40F5
Queensbury	31E1
Quellyn Lake	23D3
Quorn & Woodhouse	19C5/26G1
Quy	21G2
Radcliffe	30F2/40D1
Radcliffe Black Lane	30F2/40C1
Radcliffe Bridge	30F2/40D1
Radcliffe-on-Trent	20A5/27G3
Radford	19A5/26E1/27G2
Radlett	13E1/39C2
Radley	12B5
Radstock (GW)	10E1
Radstock (S&D)	10E1
Radway Green	25D4/40G1
Radyr	10C5
Raglan	10A3
Rainford (L&NW)	25A2/30G5/40D4
Rainford (L&Y)	25A2/30G5/40D4
Rainford Village	25A2/30G5/40D4
Rainham (Essex)	7A3/13F4/39D5
Rainham (Kent)	7B5/14G5
Rainhill	24A1/25A2/40E3
Raleigh's Cross	3B2
Rampside	29B5
Ramsbottom	30F2/40C1
Ramsden Dock	29B4
Ramsey (GN)	21E1
Ramsey (GN & GE)	21E12
Ramsey (IoM)	29E3
Ramsgate Harbour	8B2/14G1
Ramsgate Town	8B2/14G1
Ranskill	27D3
Raskelf	31B3
Ratby	69C5
Rauceby	20A2/28G5
Raunds	20F2
Raven Square	24G3
Ravenglass (Furness)	33F4
Ravenglass (R&ER)	33F4
Ravenscar	36F2
Ravensthorpe (L&NW)	31E2
Ravensthorpe (L&Y)	31E2
Ravenstonedale	34E2
Rawcliffe	27A3/31E5
Rawdon	31D1
Rawtenstall	30E2/40B1
Raydon Wood	14B4
Rayleigh	14E5
Rayne	13C5
Raynes Park	7B1/13G2/39E2
Raynham Park	21B5
Reading (GW)	12F3
Reading (SE&C)	12F3
Rearsby	20C5
Red House	17B4
Red Rock	30F4/40C3
Redbourn	13D1/39B2
Redbridge	5D3
Redbrook	10A2
Redcar	36D5
Reddish (L&NW)	30G2
Reddish (S&MJt)	30G2
Redditch	19F2
Redheugh Goods	35A4
Redhill	6A1/7C1/39G3
Redland	10D1
Redmile	20A4
Redmire	35G2
Rednal	24F2/25F1
Redruth	1A3/1F1
Reedham	22D2
Reednesss	27A4/31E5
Reedsmouth	38G5
Reepham (Lincs)	28E5
Reepham (Norfolk)	22C4
Reigate	6A1/7C1/39G3
Repton & Willington	19B3/26F3
Resolven	9B4/16F3
Reston	37A5
Retford	27D3
Retford Goods (GC)	27D4
Rhayader	16A2/17C4
Rhewl	24C4
Rhiwderyn	10C4
Rhoose	10D5
Rhos	24D3/25E1
Rhos Tryfan	23C3
Rhosgoch	23A2
Rhostyllen	24D2/25D1
Rhuddlan	24B4
Rhydneredydd	24F3/25F1
Rhydowen	15D3
Rhydryonen	17A1/23G4
Rhydymwyn	24C3/40F5
Rhyl	24B5
Rhymney (B&M)	10A5/16E1
Rhymney (Rhymney)	10A5/16E1
Rhymney Bridge	10A5/16E1
Ribblehead	34G2/30A3
Ribbleton	30D4/40B3
Riccall	31D4
Riccarton	37F3
Richmond (N. Yorks)	35F3
Richmond (Surrey)	13G1/39E2
Rickmansworth (L&NW)	12E1/39C1
Rickmansworth (Metropolitan)	12E1/39C1
Riddings	37G2
Ridgmont	12B1
Riding Mill	35B2
Rillington	32A5
Rimington	30C2/40A1
Ringley Road	30F3/40D1
Ringstead & Addington	20F3
Ringwood	4D1/5E2
Ripley Valley	31B2
Ripley	26D2/27F1
Ripon	31A2
Rippingale	20B2
Ripple	11B1/18E1
Ripponden	30E1
Risca	10B4
Rishton	30E3/40B2
Rishworth	30E1
Roade	12A3/20G4
Roadwater	3A2/10F5
Roath	10C4
Robertsbridge	7E4
Robin Hood	27A1/31E1
Robin Hood's Bay	36F2
Roby	24A1/25B2/40E4
Rocester	19A2/26E4
Rochdale	30F2
Rochester Bridge	7B4/13G5
Rochester	7B5/13G5
Rochford	14E5
Rock Ferry	24A2/25B1/40E5